What people are saying about …

NOW OVER NEXT

"If you want to press back against the world's constant pressure to perform, get ahead, and be onto the next thing … *this book is for you.* Hope knows what it looks like to walk through exhausting seasons of striving for your worth as she leads you toward a better narrative focused on where God has planted your feet right now. This is a crucial message for women in our current culture. If you're tired and need a friend to walk with you on a journey of contentment and joy, Hope is your gal!"

Rebecca George, author of *Do the Thing* and
You're Not Too Late, host of *Radical Radiance*
podcast, and founder of Camp for Creatives

"In a world that screams for us to not miss out on anything, Hope reminds us that when we live life submitted to Jesus, we actually don't miss out on anything because He is everything. You'll find this book freeing if the pressure to prove and do is weighing on you. Filled with wisdom and authenticity, *Now Over Next* will leave you feeling confident that in the *now*, the Lord is preparing you for what is *next!*"

Allyson Golden, author of *Arise and
Shine* and *Words Are Golden*

"This is the book every girl needs in her hands. It's a reminder that, with God, you're never missing out on anything that's meant for you. This empowering message will help women everywhere ditch the fear of missing out and start appreciating what God is doing in the here

and now. Stop chasing what's next and start embracing what's now. Do yourself a favor—read this book."

Grace Valentine, author, blogger, podcast host, and speaker

"In a world that constantly tells us we're missing out, this book is a breath of fresh air. It reminds us that God has already given us everything we need—nothing less, nothing missing. With wisdom and grace, Hope fixes our eyes on freedom from the fear of scarcity and comparison and points us back to abundance in Him. A must-read for anyone longing to trust more deeply in God's perfect provision."

Rachel Awtrey, author, speaker, and podcast host of *Real Talk with Rachel Awtrey*

"Hope knows exactly how to point out the emotion we've all experienced yet struggle to name: FOMO. She gives us practical tools and spiritual encouragement to not only live in the moment but to experience freedom in the *now*."

Kim Caputo, author and podcast host

"This book is the perfect companion for any woman feeling the pressure to keep up. It reminds you that when you're walking with God, there's no such thing as missing out. Instead of constantly striving for what's next, let this message empower you to find peace and purpose right where you are. Let go of the fear of falling behind—because God's plan is unfolding in your life right now. Trust me, you'll want to read this."

Mikella Van Dyke, founder of Chasing Sacred

NOW
OVER
NEXT

Conquering the Fear
of Missing Out

NOW
OVER
NEXT

Hope Reagan Harris

ep

estherpress

Books for Courageous Women
from David C Cook

NOW OVER NEXT
Published by Esther Press,
an imprint of David C Cook
4050 Lee Vance Drive
Colorado Springs, CO 80918 U.S.A.

Integrity Music Limited, a Division of David C Cook
Brighton, East Sussex BN1 2RE, England

Esther Press®, DAVID C COOK® and related marks are
registered trademarks of David C Cook.

Unless otherwise noted, all Scripture quotations are taken from the ESV® Bible
(The Holy Bible, English Standard Version®), copyright © 2001 by Crossway,
a publishing ministry of Good News Publishers. Used by permission. All
rights reserved. MSG are taken from THE MESSAGE, copyright © 1993,
2018 by Eugene H. Peterson. Used by permission of NavPress, represented by
Tyndale House Publishers. All rights reserved; NIV are taken from the Holy
Bible, New International Version®, NIV®. Copyright © 1973, 2011 by Biblica,
Inc.™ Used by permission of Zondervan. All rights reserved worldwide. www.
zondervan.com. The "NIV" and "New International Version" are trademarks
registered in the United States Patent and Trademark Office by Biblica, Inc.™
The author has added italics and bolds to Scripture quotations for emphasis.

Library of Congress Control Number 2024943981
ISBN 978-0-8307-8587-2
eISBN 978-0-8307-8605-3

© 2025 Hope Reagan Harris
Published in association with the Books & Such Literary Management,
2222 Cleveland Ave., #1005, Santa Rosa, CA 95403, www.booksandsuch.com

The Team: Susan McPherson, Stephanie Bennett, Julie Cantrell, Judy
Gillispie, Michael Fedison, James Hershberger, Karen Sherry
Cover Design: Brian Mellema

Printed in the United States of America
First Edition 2025

1 2 3 4 5 6 7 8 9 10

110624

To Remi Claire Harris:
Since the moment we knew your name, I started
praying that you'd live up to it.
Your first name means "remedy," and your middle name means
"bright light." I prayed that your bright light would show people
Jesus and that this alone would bring healing in their lives.
Since the moment you were born, you've been doing that.
I can't even tell you how much healing you've brought in
my life—in areas I didn't even know needed healing.
This book wouldn't exist without you.
God used YOU to teach me the message inside these pages.
My sweet girly pop, I love you with my whole heart. I can't
wait to continue to learn from you and watch you change lives
with your joyous, generous, funny, sweet, and determined
spirit that He's given you. You were made for this moment.

Therefore, if anyone is in Christ, the new creation has come: The old has gone, the new is here!
2 Corinthians 5:17 NIV

Contents

Let's Invite Him In!

Hi, sweet friend,

Before you turn the page and get started, I'd love for us to say a prayer together. I truly believe that God wants to do a new thing in your life. And where He is wanted, He will *move*.

So let's invite Him in! Pray with me:

Dear God,

We come to you today and invite You into our lives and into this journey we're about to start.

Lord, will You please do a new thing within us? Will You guide us and move in our lives?

God, we want You above everything else. You are worth the cost. You are worthy of it all.

Will You give us wisdom and reveal new things to us in these pages? Will You please teach us and encourage us on this journey? Will You equip us to be bold and to take the leap of faith when opportunities arise?

We want YOU and nothing else. We invite You to do things in and through our lives that You've never partnered with us on before. Lord, we are desperate for You to move. Do what only You can do. Reveal Yourself to us and make us *new*.

Help us to see what You are doing NOW.

Help us to no longer worry about what's next or what we aren't a part of.

Help us believe that when we're walking with You, there is no such thing as missing out.

Fill us with Your Spirit. We want every single void in our lives to be filled with You.

Move through this message, and move in our lives. Thank You for this life. Thank You for your Son, Jesus.

In Jesus' name we pray, amen.

When We Know There Is More to Life Than This

They say a picture is worth a thousand words. However, if you look closely at the photo on the next page, which is from 2020, you'll see more than just twenty-six-year-old me on a business trip in India. Dressed for success in my striped button-down shirt with freshly highlighted blonde hair, I'm standing proudly in front of the Taj Mahal. The big smile on my face screams "I've arrived!" And I even posted this photo on social media with the caption: "Made it to the Taj!"

Leading up to this India trip, I had been traveling all around the world. My American Airlines status had upgraded me to first-class seats, and I was living the American Dream!

What a change from my simple small-town childhood in a community of ten thousand fellow residents. It hadn't been long since I'd

googled "Fortune 500 company" with no clue what that term even meant. But soon after I graduated from college, I would not only learn what a Fortune 500 company was, but I'd spend five years working for one. By the time this photo was taken, I had become the typical modern business leader, determined to make it to "the top of the corporate ladder."

Can you relate? Whether you've been striving in your professional, romantic, or personal life, I bet we all have "chased" some goal along the way. And I bet, if you're anything like me, you might be caught in that cycle right now.

Let's imagine we are climbing a ladder. Each rung signifies the next step we'll have to take to reach whatever goal we're striving to achieve—whether it be more money, more success, more approval, more accolades, or more time. We all keep climbing, trying to achieve MORE, MORE, MORE! Then, and only then, will we finally be happy.

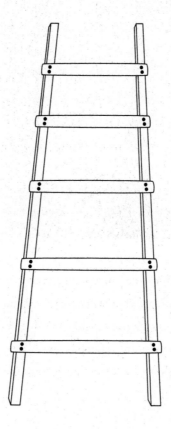

Initially, this climb can feel exhilarating. However, as we climb higher, the ladder starts swaying and wobbling. Each step feels like an empty promise, disappointing us when our expectations aren't met. We slowly begin to realize that the way our life *looks* is drastically different from how it *feels*.

When I look back at the old Hope, standing there in front of the Taj Mahal, I see a goal-driven, hardworking, and career-focused young woman who was eager to reach the next step ... and the next ... and the next ... and the next. The climb became addictive, dribbling out enough reward to keep me hooked. The more success I found, the more I wanted.

As a result, I spent years "living to work," when I should have been "working to live."

As much as I hate to admit it, I had become a workaholic, addicted to worldly success. I was rarely content with the moment I was in and spent most of my time focusing on the next step in front of me. As soon as I'd get a promotion, I'd turn right around and ask my boss what goals I needed to achieve to reach the next level.

I approached my career as if I were playing a game. It didn't matter how much striving it took; I was going to win. I was going to figure out a way to reach the next best thing that was always dangling in front of me.

Now, writing this from a new perspective, I realize it was never about the money or material things those promotions got me. I craved the praise and recognition that came along with them. Each accomplishment fueled my confidence and filled a void inside of me long enough to fuel me onward and upward as I continued to climb the ladder.

Work was where I found my worth and identity, so that's what I focused on. It made me feel relevant, known, loved, and purposeful. To put it as simply as possible: the old Hope had set her eyes on creating a success story for herself.

If we're being honest with each other, there's always something dangling in front of us that appears to promise a better, happier, or more fulfilling life. Maybe you long to graduate college, land your first job, find your person, earn a promotion at work, get married, have a baby, buy a house, start a company, purchase a new car, or ... fill in the blank. In today's culture, we're battling a universal epidemic that tries to trick us into chasing the *next best thing*. Can you take a guess what that epidemic is called?

Yes, we're talking about the "fear of missing out," or FOMO, as many call it.

Most of us have joked about "having major FOMO."

Maybe you've scrolled through social media posts and felt FOMO when you realized others were having fun without you.

Maybe you've watched your coworker accept a promotion and felt FOMO when you worried your big chance may have passed you by.

Maybe you've seen your friends marry, have babies, and build their dream homes, all while you've remained single, battling FOMO alone in your apartment and fearing you'll never catch up with your peers.

Most of us have felt this FEAR of missing out at least once in our lives, and many of us have allowed it to dictate our decisions. That's why I think it's time we take a serious look at FOMO—a false cultural belief that seems to be getting worse with each passing year.

To me, FOMO is the constant worry that if we don't keep up with what everyone else is doing, we might fall behind in life. It's the desire to be in the loop because we're afraid that not being part of the action could mean missing out on something important or exciting. And it's the desire to be everything for everyone, leading us to say yes when we really want to say no.

This fear doesn't only impact us emotionally; it impacts every part of our lives. FOMO can make us feel lonely, influence our ability to make sound decisions, increase our symptoms of depression and anxiety, and create sleep problems, which in turn will make us even more exhausted and overwhelmed. Let's not forget how it can impact our financial well-being by tricking us into spending money on things we haven't budgeted for.

The problem with FOMO is, we can become so busy trying to create a life worth living that we end up *missing out* on the present moment God has placed right in front of us.

It's time for us to embrace where God has us today. It's time to embrace NOW over NEXT.

What If We Are Holding On to What We Were Never Meant to Cling To?

Have you ever felt so caught up in trying to keep up with others that you ended up missing out on what God was doing in that very moment of your life? I have! It's no wonder my wise eighty-seven-year-old nana says, "FOMO could make us miss a blessing."

Nana understands that we can't lose sight of who God is, who He says we are, and what He promises to do with our lives. To put it

simply: In a world where people are often anything but *present*, it's time we step into the unexpected gift of abundant life Christ has given us in this very moment.

Remember that picture of the old Hope standing in front of the Taj Mahal? I look happy, successful, living the dream! But my prayer journal entries from that time in my life captured truths the photo would have never told you:

> *Something has to change. I'm feeling especially tired and weary … There has to be more to life than this … I'm exhausted, burned out, and wishing for retirement in my twenties … All night I felt restless and anxious about work. This truly feels imprisoning … God, I am literally at my wit's end. I'm extremely overwhelmed … I lay this all at Your feet, Lord. I seriously want to point people to You. That's my heart.*

Can you see the hold FOMO had on my life at that time? FOMO holds us hostage and convinces us to keep climbing (even if the climb is making us ill). It manipulates us, saying, *Why would you stop here? You're almost to the good part! If you quit climbing, others will pass you up!*

There Is More to Life Than This

Before 2020, I had been looking at life through a foggy lens. But in 2020, the fog began to clear. My perspective was starting to shift as I realized that *maybe* there was more to life than climbing

the corporate ladder. But I wasn't ready to make big adjustments in my life just yet.

If this sounds like your current situation, don't feel bad. If God met me there, He will meet you there too. The fact that you are even thinking there *might* be a better approach to life is a GREAT start. This is the place where I started to get to know God by praying and reading my Bible. I learned very quickly that the process is a *journey* (which transforms us little by little each day), not a sprint.

While still working in my corporate job, I decided on a whim to see what other career opportunities were out there. Burned out and longing for a better balance in life, I applied for my dream role in digital ministry, but when I learned it would require me to move to Oklahoma City, I withdrew my application. A cross-country relocation was not in the cards for our family.

Even though I withdrew my application, the hiring manager, Ben, reached out to have a chat. We each had a corporate background, and he wanted to learn more about what had led me to apply and what I was wrestling with in terms of the position. We agreed to stay connected, and we emailed each other two or three times a year. (This detail may seem random, but wait to see what God does with this!)

Three years later, the fog that once clouded my vision had finally lifted. My firstborn baby, Remi Claire, was born on January 19, and as most mothers understand, my entire world changed.

I finally understood that there was *definitely* more to life than chasing after every step society told me to take. The things I used to work hard for didn't fill me up anymore. In all honesty, corporate achievements now felt meaningless.

Work still went on while I was on maternity leave. I knew it would, but it felt weird. I wasn't getting calls in the evenings to help solve "mission critical" problems at work. I wasn't being asked to pull together last-minute presentations. I wasn't being praised or acknowledged for my job performance. In fact, I was on maternity leave during our company's review process, so I wasn't even able to have my annual review, a process I'd previously looked forward to as an opportunity to spotlight my achievements and climb another level up that ladder.

My time at home with Remi gave me enough space to process the way I had been living since entering corporate America in 2017. I finally accepted that enough was enough.

This much-needed shift created a moment of clarity, and I never saw life the same way again.

Suddenly, the shiny steps on the ladder lost their sparkle. I came eye to eye with all the things I had sacrificed to keep up with the climb.

Of course, transcendence never comes easy. And if it had, I wouldn't even have a story to share with you today. The truth is, life caught up with me and did everything it could to try to knock me down.

Sound relatable?

Ten weeks after giving birth to Remi, I was diagnosed with postpartum depression. For the first time in my entire life, I couldn't keep it together. I also could no longer pretend everything was fine. I wasn't fine, not even close. And I had no choice but to surrender fully to God.

This wasn't the only shocking news that was delivered to me that day. You're going to chuckle a little ... but a few weeks before

Remi came into the world, I'd applied for a promotion within my department. While I was sitting on my couch that evening, trying to process my diagnosis, I got a text from a coworker. Turns out, she had applied for the same job, and the hiring manager had recommended she reach out to me for interview advice.

It didn't take thirty seconds for me to realize this wasn't a good sign. Reluctantly, I texted her back. Even though I had no clue what God was up to, I chose to trust His plan.

A few days later, that peer reached out to me again, this time to notify me that she had been given the position over me. I had been told I was a shoo-in for that promotion. And just like that, I could do nothing but congratulate her as that door slammed in my face.

To make matters worse, I wasn't able to reach any closure or apply for any other positions at my company until my maternity leave ended. After all the time, energy, and attention I had poured into that company, I was devastated that my climb had been stopped at a time when I had NO control over the decisions being made without me.

Even though I had no clue what God was up to, I chose to trust His plan.

Depressed, anxious, sleep-deprived, and frustrated, I had no choice but to surrender not only this career situation but my entire life over to God. I had to accept that I was not in control. And that I never had been. I needed God to show me what He had in store for

me since I felt certain it wasn't the next step on that corporate ladder anymore.

If You're on the Wrong Ladder, It's Time to Step Off

We all know the higher we climb, the greater the risk. However, climbing down can be just as hard, if not harder, than the ascent. One wrong step and we're doomed … or at least that's what FOMO tells us.

What if we take a misstep on our way down?
What if we regret abandoning our climb?
What if all our hard work was for nothing?

Striving was the name of the game I had been playing for years. I'd given everything to climbing that corporate ladder, and I admit … I was afraid to give it up. The thought of letting go of my career gave me butterflies.

I would snuggle Remi as she slept and try to think of every alternative way to make a living.

Maybe I could launch a coaching business?
Perhaps I could become a public speaker?
Should I start a stationery company?

Yes, it may all seem ridiculous now, but I considered *every* angle as a possible solution. Still, each idea felt like I was trying to step into

a place where I didn't belong. It soon became clear that the next step on my old ladder was no longer meant to be *my* next step.

I was tired of being strapped to this unstable ladder, defining my worth by worldly success, accomplishments, and accolades. I had been hanging on by a thread for a long time, and the thread had finally broken.

With sudden clarity, I could see that each next step was nothing more than an illusion of security. How had I fallen for the scheme?

FOMO had been *keeping me stuck* in the middle of something I was never supposed to be a part of in the first place. In fact, FOMO had not only led me to climb the wrong ladder; it had stopped me from stepping off the ladder and stepping into the abundant life the Bible tells us about.

> *If you're on the wrong ladder, there is never a better time to step off than now.*

It was time to stop the striving. It was time to shift perspective.

Jesus says in John 10:10 that the thief wants to "steal and kill and destroy" but Jesus came so that we "may have life and have it abundantly." Have you ever become so busy trying to secure the next best thing that you end up missing out on the moment God has you in? I had become so afraid of "missing out" on achieving MORE, MORE, MORE that I had actually been missing out on the blessings God had already given me.

Letting Go of the Way of the World

A call to my husband, Will, solidified my decision. It was time to descend this corporate ladder once and for all. He stood by me, assuring me that we would navigate this transition together and that everything would be okay—even if it meant significant sacrifices.

A few days after this conversation (and a lot of prayer), I was losing hope again. Discouraged, angry, and exhausted, I prayed for God to help me through the struggle, to give me clarity about next steps, and to help me surrender fully to His will for my life.

Then, the Bible's story of David inspired me to believe I didn't have to figure this all out on my own. Are you familiar with this story?

God told the prophet Samuel to anoint the next king: one of Jesse's sons. So Samuel went to find this new king. After seeing all the other brothers, Samuel asked if there were any sons he hadn't seen yet. Jesse was reluctant to admit he had another son, as even he didn't believe in David. But despite no one thinking David was the right man for the job, Samuel discovered this outcast son tending the sheep, exactly where God had placed him.

Let's take a look at how David was discovered:

> So he asked Jesse, "Are these all the sons you have?"
>
> "There is still the youngest," Jesse answered. "He is tending the sheep."
>
> Samuel said, "Send for him; we will not sit down until he arrives."

So he sent for him and had him brought in.
He was glowing with health and had a fine appearance and handsome features.
Then the LORD said, "Rise and anoint him;
this is the one." (1 Samuel 16:11–12 NIV)

Do you see what happened here? God sought out a lowly shep-
herd boy, a boy who was *not* focused on climbing the wrong "ladder,"
a boy who was not pouring all his energy into achieving accolades
and accomplishments. Then, God (not David) made a way for this
obedient servant to be anointed as the future king.

If God made a way for David, He can do surprising things in our
lives too. Once I realized the real meaning of this familiar story, I
cried out to God and said, "Please send someone to find me like you
sent Samuel to find David!"

We've all heard that truth is stranger than fiction. Well, in my
case, this age-old saying certainly held up, because I couldn't possibly
make up what happened next.

As I was holding ten-week-old Remi Claire in my kitchen and
catching up on emails, I found an unexpected message in my inbox.
It had arrived around the same time I'd prayed for God to send
someone to find me. The subject line was titled "Visiting Rogers,"
and guess who it was from? Ben from the digital ministry company!
(Remember him?)

Turns out, he was planning to visit my hometown and suggested
we meet at my favorite local coffee shop. See? If God has done it
before, He can do it again.

When the time came to connect in person, Ben and I spent extensive time chatting about how FOMO had prevented me from putting in my two-week notice so that I could resign from my corporate job.

"If you're on the wrong ladder, there is never a better time to step off than now," Ben said.

> I had become so afraid of "missing out" on achieving MORE, MORE, MORE that I had actually been missing out on the blessings God had already given me.

I sat speechless, stunned at the way God had chosen to deliver this very clear message to me. Still, the descent is scary. The way FOMO stifles us is no joke. But I had stalled long enough. The time had come for me to step off the wrong ladder. I was ready to discover what God had prepared for me.

God Is Worth Selling Out To

While facing this inner struggle, I found comfort from a strange, unforgettable dream. I was in a random house with seven door openings, but no actual doors. When I went on the hunt to find the doors that fit in these spaces, I discovered seven black doors. This is where it gets weird.

When I went to install them, they didn't fit like a typical door. I kept trying to put them in like a normal door, and they wouldn't work. The only way to install them was upside down.

After I finished installing them, I looked through one of the doors' windows. Guess what I saw.

Remi and me holding hands in a field and reveling in the simplicity of life.

I wasn't scrambling to come up with the next best business idea or working to the point of exhaustion to get promoted. I was living in the moment and embracing the season of motherhood that God had me in right now.

It's impossible to miss out when our eyes are focused on God and our identity is found in Him.

As I shared this unusual dream with my mom, she told me about Matthew 13:44, which reads: "God's kingdom is like a treasure hidden in a field for years and then accidentally found by a trespasser. The finder is ecstatic—what a find!—and proceeds to sell everything he owns to raise money and buy that field" (MSG).

Once we get a taste of the unexpected gift found in the moment that God offers us right now, everything changes for us. Sacrifices start to give us joy. Trials start to fire us up for what God must be up to. Serving others becomes our mission.

We start to see that we don't have to worry about the next big thing. We start to see that we have everything we need right now. We start to see that it's impossible to miss out when our eyes are focused on God and our identity is found in Him. We start to see that everything we have was never ours to hold onto. We start to make bold moves that the world would consider crazy or even delusional. We start to believe that each step off this ladder is one step closer to the abundant life God has waiting for us.

Clinging to the Promises of God

I had exactly three weeks of maternity leave left when Ben connected me with several leaders at the digital ministry company. I had devoted YEARS of my life to serving the other company, a company that had passed me up for promotion without even having a personal conversation about it. But, once again, I was learning that God is always right on time. *I only needed to give my employer a two-week notice, and that was the exact timing in which His next step was revealed to me.*

Not only was I was offered my dream ministry position, but I wouldn't have to relocate for the job. They were giving me a REMOTE position! This wasn't a role I could do with Remi at home, but it was a role that would allow me to maximize my time with her and still have a career. We had a daycare ten minutes down the road with a spot secured for her. I would drop her off around nine o'clock in the morning, and Will's mom would get her after lunch and watch her until I got off work later that afternoon.

Even though the timing was a God thing and the logistics with Remi were falling into place nicely, Will and I still had a tough decision to make for our family. In full transparency, FOMO hit hard. Would I continue climbing that old career ladder? Or could I bravely step into the new position God was calling me to?

After giving me the remote job offer, the hiring manager said, "All you have to do is decide if you are called or not. Don't let the details stop you. If you are called, say yes and trust that God will work everything else out."

While the risks were many, Will and I decided to make a leap of faith. We were ready to trust that God had something planned for our family on the other side of my corporate climb. We knew there was more to life than the way I had been living, and we were ready to see what God was going to do through this next step in my faith journey.

It turns out that what often looks like a step back can really be a giant hop forward. Matthew 6:33 says, "Seek first his kingdom and his righteousness, and all these things will be given to you as well" (NIV).

God promises not to fail us. He tells us again and again that we can step away from FEAR and put our FAITH in Him:

- He will be with us wherever we go (Joshua 1:9).
- He has plans for us (Jeremiah 29:11).
- He will renew our strength (Isaiah 40:31).
- He has made a way to spend eternity with us (John 4:14).
- He will bless our obedience to Him (Psalm 1:1–3).
- He gives us comfort (2 Corinthians 1:3–4).

- He has tomorrow taken care of (Matthew 6:25–34).
- He will give us rest (Matthew 11:28).
- He is preparing a place for us and will come back for us (John 14:2–3).
- He will use every circumstance and situation in our lives for His good (Romans 8:28).
- He gives us peace that often doesn't make sense because of what we're walking through (Philippians 4:6–7).
- He will fight for us (Exodus 14:14).

God will keep His word and lead us to experience fulfillment right NOW. Here's to our journey of discovering what it really means to choose NOW over NEXT.

Embrace the Now

1. What does FOMO mean to you?

2. How does FOMO make you feel?

3. Have you had a moment when you said to yourself that there has to be more to life than the way you're living today?

4. Have you ever become so busy trying to secure a certain life that you end up missing out on experiencing the moment you're in?

5. How would you describe the "ladder" you've been climbing and the next rung you've been striving to step onto?

6. What do you believe God will do in your life NOW?

Chapter 2

When We're Ready to Conquer the Fear of Missing Out

God never works the way we expect. In fact, His way is always better than what we would have planned for ourselves.

You probably have no idea how God is going to use you right where you are today, but I believe it is going to be better than anything you can picture.

I honestly thought that when I stepped into the new ministry job, everything would feel different. I had made a major shift in my external life, and I thought a major shift would happen internally as well. I don't know why I thought this, but I believed this new job was going to automatically fix my striving, my depression, my sleepless nights.

But the old Hope came with me to the new job. I cringe a little as I write this because I haven't said this out loud to anyone. It's a

little truth I've kept hidden because it exposes my heart in a way I don't like and I'm definitely not proud of.

When I started the position, my boss had me drive to their office in Oklahoma City for my first week on the job. I'll never forget going to lunch with my new teammates. I was sure to tell them about the teams I had led, the global traveling I had done, and how I planned to add value in my new role. I wanted them to be impressed with my experience and excited that I was joining their company.

Then, I ended my story by saying that people thought I was crazy for leaving my high-paying leadership position in the corporate world but that I knew what looked like a setback to the world was God's way of setting me up to experience His best for me.

I remember thinking, *Did I really let it slip to my new teammates that I feel like this new job is a setback?* With grace, everyone at the table acted like I hadn't said that, and they went on to share their stories of how they started working in that ministry.

Turns out, I wasn't the only one who had sacrificed something that mattered to me to step into this job. The only real difference between us was they showed much more humility than me.

As I left that day, I reflected on the conversation. Why were my striving tendencies popping right back up? I thought this new job was going to lead to a new me ... but the old Hope seemed to be coming into this new place with me.

Now that I look back on it, I can clearly see that FOMO still had a hold on me. I was having a hard time letting go of the title I used to have, the brand I had created for myself in corporate America, and the executive track I had been on. I knew God had something *more*

for me than the way I had been living, but releasing my old patterns and beliefs proved excruciatingly painful.

I was Hope, the girl whose executive mentors had seen something in, the girl whose future had promised a C-suite title, the girl with experience across seven different areas of the business, and the girl who was every boss's favorite because she would work late hours or weekends and take on more than she could handle to seek their approval. Sadly, that Hope wasn't going anywhere anytime soon.

It was weird, but for some reason talking about it made me feel like I was still living it. It was a way of holding on to what I had accomplished and trying to control what people thought of me in this new job.

I hope you read this somewhat cringey truth of mine and experience a sigh of relief. If you, too, feel like letting go and stepping into the new is happening at a turtle's pace, you're in good company. **The key goal in this chapter is for us to get comfortable with the fact that transformation takes time. It doesn't happen overnight, and that's beautiful.**

The Life of a Butterfly

We aren't the only ones God designed to transform over a period of time. Let's look at the life cycle of a monarch butterfly as an example.

The life cycle of a butterfly, known as metamorphosis, has four parts: egg, larva, pupa, and adult. This transformation process takes about a month and looks a little something like this:

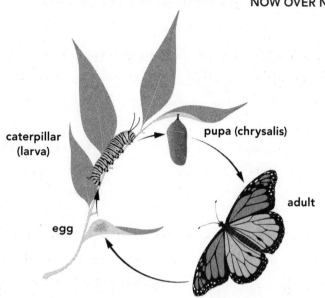

caterpillar (larva)

pupa (chrysalis)

adult

egg

A butterfly starts off as an **egg**. It remains in this stage for four to six days before it hatches. Once the butterfly hatches, it emerges as a **caterpillar (larva)**.

At this stage, the caterpillar has two main functions: eat and grow. It stays close to its food source (milkweed) and sheds its skin each time it outgrows it.

In about two weeks, when the caterpillar is fully grown, it leaves the milkweed and finds a new, safe place to become a **pupa**. At this point, the caterpillar creates a silk-like mat, attaches itself to it, hangs upside down, and sheds its skin one last time, this time trading it for a bright green casting called a chrysalis.

While it is inside the **chrysalis**, key transformations take place over a period of eight to twelve days. Then, the chrysalis cracks open and the **butterfly** enters the world. Once free, it doesn't immediately fly. Instead, it clings to its chrysalis until the wings can expand and dry. Then, in God's perfect timing, the butterfly flies away.

Let's do some math here. The adult butterfly lives on average for two weeks. So, let's say this butterfly lives forty-three days total.

Egg = 5 days
Larva = 14 days
Chrysalis = 10 days
Butterfly = 14 days

In this butterfly's life, 67 percent of its days were spent preparing to be the butterfly that God was transforming it to be. That's the majority of its life! The transformation of a butterfly doesn't happen overnight, and our transformation doesn't happen overnight either.

The Butterfly in You

I haven't met a girl who doesn't love butterflies. There is something so beautiful about them. It doesn't matter what they are doing; they catch our attention.

The transformation process that a butterfly goes through is called **metamorphosis**. According to Webster's dictionary, *metamorphosis* means "a striking alteration in appearance, character, or circumstances."* I'm not sure where you are in your journey of transformation with God, but I know He is doing a work in and through you.

Let's consider two key facts about the caterpillar or larva stage:

---

* *Merriam-Webster Dictionary*, s.v. "metamorphosis," www.merriam-webster.com/dictionary/metamorphosis.

1. Caterpillars don't see well and may not even be able to see the difference between day and night.
2. They fill themselves up with the food from their immediate environment, milkweed.

Now, let's think about our transformational journeys. When we first stepped on our ladders, we were like caterpillars. We couldn't see beyond our immediate environment. We climbed like there wasn't any other way of life. Even if we had tried to see it differently in the beginning, we wouldn't have been able to. We, like the caterpillars, couldn't see there was more to life than the way we were living.

The caterpillars ate the food where they were placed. Did you feed off things the ladder offered you?

I know I definitely did. I ate up the *atta-girls*. Each promotion gave me the energy and motivation I needed to keep climbing. The things of this world appeared to be solid ground, and, like that caterpillar, I had no idea I was actually clinging to something that wasn't stable at all.

Now, let's consider what happened when that caterpillar turned into a chrysalis. As it grew, it shed its old skin, not just once, but over and over again.

Like the caterpillar, each step we took on the ladder grew us and stretched us to shed a little bit of who we once were. We could start to see that the things that once fulfilled us weren't as solid as we thought. We started to have a hunch that there might be more to life than the next rung on the ladder.

What happened next in the butterfly's life? It continued to grow until it realized it was time to leave the only environment it had

known, milkweed. Then it set out to find a new place and start the process of becoming a chrysalis.

How does a caterpillar know when it's time to turn into a chrysalis? Its juvenile hormone levels drop to a low level, signaling it's time for the next stage of development.

Think about this: Climbing our old ladder was a bit like munching on milkweed. It made us feel good. It filled us. It sustained us. It kept us dangling from an unstable surface, climbing for the next level that would deliver a reward to us. No matter how much we "ate," we wanted more.

Then, what happened? Something shifted internally. We could see the ladder we were on for what it was. We had outgrown the very place we had spent so much time and energy striving to reach … only to reach it and want off of the unstable place we were standing on.

> *Jesus is the only way to step into our new, true identity.*

Here's another interesting fact about the butterfly's metamorphosis: The caterpillar hangs upside down in its chrysalis, curling its body into the shape of the letter J. Isn't that fascinating? The only way it can experience metamorphosis and become the butterfly it was born to be is by surrendering to the J!

To me, that J represents Jesus. Jesus is the safe place where we can rest. Jesus is the mandatory step in our transformation journey.

The only way to become the people we were born to be is through Jesus.

Jesus is the WAY.

Jesus articulates this beautifully in John 15:4: "Live in me. Make your home in me just as I do in you. In the same way that a branch can't bear grapes by itself but only by being joined to the vine, you can't bear fruit unless you are joined with me" (MSG).

Jesus tells us the only way to experience the wondrous metamorphosis process in our own lives is to make our home in Him. He is the only one with the ability to miraculously transform our hearts and change the trajectory of our lives.

It's Heart Transformation, Not Behavior Modification

Looking back at my actions when I first stepped off my corporate ladder and stepped into my new dream job, I can clearly see that I was searching for my safe place to grow and transform. Of course, I had it all wrong. I thought my safe place was a physical location. I thought my safe place was this new job with this incredible environment of Christian peers. I thought a physical change in career would result in a spiritual change inside me.

You've probably already figured out that this "quick fix" didn't work out quite as I'd expected.

I didn't realize it at the time, but I had simply shifted striving for career accomplishments to striving for transformation. I became frustrated that a true transformation wasn't happening on my schedule.

I hope you don't have to learn this the hard way like me, but heart transformation doesn't rely on our own strength ... no matter how hard we try. I tried to speed up the transformation process. I wanted to be different overnight. But Jesus reminded me I wasn't the one in control here.

Jesus continues in John 15 by saying,

> I am the Vine, you are the branches. When you're joined with me and I with you, the relation intimate and organic, the harvest is sure to be abundant. Separated, you can't produce a thing. Anyone who separates from me is deadwood, gathered up and thrown on the bonfire. But if you make yourselves at home with me and my words are at home in you, you can be sure that whatever you ask will be listened to and acted upon. This is how my Father shows who he is—when you produce grapes, when you mature as my disciples. (vv. 5–8 MSG)

My heart was in the right place, but I wasn't staying connected to Jesus. I was trying to run ahead of Him and step into the new, beautiful butterfly version of me in my own timing. If Jesus Himself tells us we have to join Him, then that is what we'd better do.

Jesus is the *only* way to experience true transformation—transformation that changes the heart from the inside out.

Jesus + nothing = everything.

The Bible gives us a transformation story involving a man named Saul. Saul started out as a guy the Christians feared. He was known to hunt down Christians and put them in prison. His mission was to stop the spread of Jesus (Acts 8).

One day, while Saul was on his way to round up more Christians, he encountered Jesus, and his life began to change. Take a look at his metamorphosis:

1. Saul encountered Jesus while he was on his way to persecute Christians (Acts 9:1–6).
2. No longer fulfilled by how he had been living, Saul became filled with the Holy Spirit, the same Spirit who rose Jesus from the dead (Acts 9:17).
3. As a public sign of his heart's transformation, Saul was baptized (Acts 9:18).
4. Saul traveled to Arabia to spend time alone with Jesus (Galatians 1:15–17).
5. Saul preached the gospel and proclaimed Jesus' name, but people were skeptical of his new "agenda" (Acts 9:20–30).
6. The Holy Spirit continued to lead Saul to share the Good News, giving him a new identity and changing his name from Saul to Paul as an outward symbol of his inner transformation (Acts 13:4–12).
7. Paul embarked on missions, sharing the gospel wherever God sent him. Paul's faith did not come without a cost.

As a result of preaching God's Word, he experienced deep suffering, imprisonments, beatings, and trials. But his unwavering faith made him strong and steadfast, even during severe persecution (2 Corinthians 11:23–27; Philippians 1:12–14).

8. Paul became known as one of the most influential figures in early Christianity. Still today, we are encouraged and challenged by his transformation journey and his unshakable faith.

We see through the story of Saul that when we're prepared to release our past pursuits and declare Jesus as our Lord and Savior, we undergo a soul-deep transformation. But Saul could have never become Paul without spending time alone with Jesus.

Jesus is the only way to step into our new, true identity.

Just as Jesus renamed Saul and gave him a new identity, I believe He stands ready to do a new thing in and through YOU.

Released Means "Set Free"

Shortly after joining the ministry team, my friend CC invited me as a guest on her podcast to share what God had been doing in my life. During the interview, I opened up about the old Hope who had been striving for success and how God had provided another way forward for me. I talked about stepping off of the corporate ladder I had been climbing and taking a new dream role in ministry.

I shared how Jesus had allowed me to see that a life worth living is not a life that strives for the next, but a surrendered life that lives for NOW.

After the interview was over, I knew there was one thing I needed to do to fully surrender my entire life to Jesus. I decided I wanted to be rebaptized. When I got really honest with myself, I knew in my heart that I had first been baptized at a young age because I thought I needed to do it. Looking back, I'm not sure I really understood the concept of sin or salvation at that time.

The only thing really stopping me in the past from getting rebaptized was what others might think. This new Hope didn't care about that anymore. I texted the girl at church who was in charge of the baptisms and signed up. Will knew I had been wrestling with this decision for a while, so I called him and asked if he would be the one to baptize me. He said yes!

Like Saul/Paul, I wanted to take my faith public. I wanted to show the whole world I wasn't the "old Hope," sold out to her corporate career. I was the "new Hope," sold out to Jesus and ready to be transformed by Him from the inside out.

The day I got rebaptized was so special. My friend Aren (who shared her story in *Purpose Doesn't Pause*) was visiting from Dallas, Texas, which made it extra sweet. I'll never forget walking down to the baptism pool holding hands with Will. We were in the water with believers of all ages—kids, teenagers, college students, and adults—each of us giving our lives to Jesus.

When I walked into the center of the pool with Will, I focused on Aren holding Remi in the front of the crowd. Then I was asked if

I would give my entire life to Jesus and proclaim Him as my Lord and Savior. Through tears, I said yes.

Will held me as I went under water. This moment symbolized so much more to me than words can explain. I was saying goodbye to the old Hope. I was ready to fully release control, cling to Jesus, and begin my true spiritual transformation.

When I came back out of the water, I hugged Will and couldn't stop crying. I had finally surrendered my life to Jesus, and it was time to live a surrendered life. This moment marked me. I was officially done with trying to do life all on my own.

Will left the pool first and grabbed my hand to steadily help me reenter the world. It's hard to articulate how it felt to take the first step toward this new way of living. From that moment onward, I would focus on NOW over NEXT.

Choosing to be rebaptized was no easy leap for me. It took engaging in a lot of private moments with Jesus, writing prayers in my journal, sharing conversations with other believers, and telling God each day that I wanted to give Him my life.

The only solution I kept coming to was that Jesus + nothing = everything.

Whether your next step is a public baptism or a private prayer, it is time to go all in. Maybe you've already given your life to Jesus. Or maybe this is your first time going *all in* with your faith. Either way, *both* places are reasons to celebrate. And you're right where you're supposed to be NOW.

Embrace the Now

1. What achievements or titles or relationships have you found difficult to let go of? Why have they been hard to let go of?

2. Do you also struggle with what other people think? How so?

3. What is one verse you can focus on when you start struggling with having control over your life?

4. In what ways have you noticed that true transformation in your life takes time? Can you relate this to the butterfly's metamorphosis process described in the text?

5. What are some steps you can take to stay connected to Jesus in your daily life?

Chapter 3

When We Invite Jesus into Our Daily Life

The moments with Jesus that follow our surrender are private, intimate moments that most people will never know about or see. These private moments shape our hearts and serve as a testimony of His restoration, kindness, and goodness.

I didn't always understand why it was important to make Jesus a part of my daily life. Sure, people talked about how important it was, but I had no idea where to start. I hope you find comfort in the fact that you don't have to have life all figured out in order to do life with Jesus.

Growing up, I basically said the same prayer every night at dinner: "Dear Father in heaven, thank You for this day. Thank You for my family. Thank You for this food. Please be with us the rest of the week. In Jesus' name, amen."

Confession: That was the *only* prayer I prayed until the age of twenty-three. (Gasp!) Outwardly, others knew I loved Jesus. I attended church. I talked the talk. I even pretended to walk the walk. But the truth is ... I didn't understand how to have a personal relationship with Jesus.

I had grown up believing I had to be "perfect" for Jesus to love me. So, like many Christians, I prioritized trying to do all the "right things." I tried to look like I had it all together, mainly to avoid being judged, shunned, or gossiped about by fellow churchgoers. I prioritized what people could see on the outside—works and actions. Ironically, works and actions are a result of striving. Works and actions are in *our* control.

Like every single human to walk the planet, I did commit sin. But when I did, I felt so much shame from slipping up that I kept my sin hidden. I didn't realize that Jesus was my safe place and I could run to Him with everything I was going through. My public life and my private life looked very different. I know people thought I had it all together because that is the exact picture I tried to paint. I was a striver. A doer. A people pleaser. A performer. And I had learned to put on a very good "show."

Externally, I did what I thought everyone wanted me to do. But in my private life, I stayed stuck in the same sin patterns and kept them a secret. Sin ruled my secret place, not Jesus.

If you find yourself here today, please know it's okay. This was my starting place too. If you're reading this and thinking, *Well, Hope, I'm in a place that's even worse than this*, then that's okay too. There is no benefit to feeling ashamed, no matter where you are starting. Everyone has to have a starting point.

Jesus isn't going to say, "Where have you been?" He says, "I'm so glad you're back! You have no idea how much I've missed you. My love for you never ever changes."

He is writing a story that will change the trajectory of your life *and* the lives around *you*.

Shortcuts Only Offer Temporary Relief

Our culture today glorifies shortcuts. We want to find the latest "life hack" that will move us from point A to point B as quickly as possible. We want the next big thing *today*, and we don't always care how we get there. On the flip side of getting from point A to point B, we also want time to rest and relax. We want to be entertained, taken care of, and fulfilled.

Confession: I have a guilty pleasure of watching *Selling Sunset* on Netflix. There is nothing about that show that honors Jesus, but when I'm tired after a long day it's an easy way to numb my mind and escape reality for a bit. Sometimes I binge-watch the show until I fall asleep.

This behavior ends up stealing time I could spend with Jesus.

Now I'm not saying we shouldn't ever watch television. But the choices we make each day really do matter. Shortcuts are temporary. Private moments with Jesus are lasting.

Here's an example. I started playing soccer in tenth grade. If you've ever played, you know it's a game with a lot of running. If you had ranked my skills with others on the team, I would have been ranked the worst by far. No specific skill set me apart, but I could run for days. I loved running, and I was able to keep going even after the more skilled players were at the end of their rope.

Unlike me, a fellow teammate was naturally gifted at the sport. She could score like no other, and she made it look effortless. Coach Young knew running would condition us for the games ahead, so he insisted we run laps around the high school's football field.

One day, this star player stayed at the back of the group, eventually falling a full lap behind the rest of us. When those of us in the front were on our last lap, she had a choice to make. Would she stop with us? Or would she finish her final lap?

She stopped.

You might be thinking, *Come on, Hope; it was practice.* And you'd be right. But there's a lesson here—shortcuts offer temporary relief. I loved her, but she didn't do this once. She always chose to take the shortcut. In the moment, the shortcut felt good, but it impacted her during game time.

At game time, she would often have to take breaks on the bench due to muscle cramps. She was our star player, and our entire team was impacted each time she stepped out of the game.

That's the thing about shortcuts. They don't only impact us; they impact the people around us. God placed us where we are today to love Him and love the people around us. Shortcuts keep us on the sidelines.

After high school, I hadn't exactly kept up with running or conditioning. But while studying abroad in Switzerland, I decided to run a half marathon. Pepperdine University's program gave us three-day weekends to explore different countries. Then we'd be booked with classes the rest of each week. Needless to say, I took a shortcut and chose to believe I didn't have time to train.

Another thing about shortcuts is that they show our priorities. We think shortcuts are secrets, but eventually, the private decisions are seen by those around us.

As I was running the race to celebrate my twentieth birthday, something didn't feel right. Not only had I failed to prepare for the race, but I had also eaten only an apple that morning. No training and not filling myself with the proper nutrition was a disaster waiting to happen. I knew I shouldn't have continued, but that old striver/competitor in me didn't want to give up. The old Hope surely didn't want to miss out on finishing the race and grabbing that big reward so I could add another accomplishment to my list and boost my ego up another notch. All my classmates were waiting for me at the finish line. What would they think if I quit? We had plans to celebrate my victory!

Shortcuts are temporary. Private moments with Jesus are lasting.

Just as the shortcuts had caught up with my soccer teammate years earlier, now my shortcuts were catching up with me. I passed out as soon as I saw the finish line. The medical team wheeled me across the finish line, and I remained unconscious for thirty minutes. I woke up on a stretcher in a medical tent with doctors speaking French. Then, instead of celebrating with friends, as planned, I spent the rest of my evening in the emergency room. Lesson learned!

Private Moments with Jesus Set Us Free

Earlier, we were discussing the life cycle of a butterfly, examining what happens when a caterpillar enters the solid green chrysalis.

When a caterpillar goes inside the chrysalis, something wild happens. The caterpillar digests itself and dissolves its tissues. It morphs into a soup-like form. (Ick!)

The only pieces of a caterpillar that don't turn to mush are the cells that will become the butterfly's eyes, wings, legs, and so on. Once again, the hormone levels trigger the final stage of metamorphosis. Every detail was planned as part of the divine design.

Let's not forget this all happens while the caterpillar is connected to the vine or branch—the place it deemed safe. If God is this detailed and purposeful about the transformation of a caterpillar into a butterfly, how much more detailed and purposeful is He with our transformation?

Not Everyone Is Going to See What Jesus Is Doing with You

We have seen caterpillars and butterflies many times, but we rarely see a chrysalis. This stage of the caterpillar's transformation reminds me of the importance of doing life with Jesus in the everyday, private moments.

In a world where we have access to know what most people are doing every single day and who they're doing it with, it's easy to experience FOMO when we see we weren't invited to someone's birthday party, baby shower, or wedding. We experience FOMO when we see we weren't picked or thought of for a certain

opportunity with someone. We experience FOMO when we see our friend hanging out with their significant other when we're alone.

But we all know there's a lot happening that isn't seen.

We have to get comfortable not being able to see everything God is doing within us. We also have to get comfortable with everyone else not being able to see what God is doing within us. All we have to do is remain close to Jesus and allow Him to do the work within us, even if that work is taking place in quiet, secret moments that no one else can see.

This contrasts sharply with what the world tells us—that we need to be seen and known. The world pressures us with FOMO, leading us to believe that if we're not visible or recognized by those around us, we're somehow irrelevant or unloved. Of course, that message is far from true. Abiding with Jesus often means spending many moments with Him in places and times that no one will ever even know about.

> All we have to do is remain close to Jesus and allow Him to do the work within us, even if that work is taking place in quiet, secret moments that no one else can see.

We have to reset our focus on Him and be okay with stepping into a journey that we don't have to share or explain every single detail of. Over and over again, I've caught myself trying so hard to explain on Instagram what God is doing in me. When I can't put

words to it, I get so frustrated. He has been teaching me that some things are only between Jesus and me.

When we desire to be seen, known, and heard, we can rest knowing that He sees us, knows us, and hears us. We don't have to explain everything happening inside us. We just have to let Him work in us.

God's sense of humor is unmatched. Here He was teaching me—a girl named Hope—that the cure to being unfazed by the seen things hinges on where we place our HOPE. Hebrews 11:1 says, "Now faith is the assurance of things hoped for, the conviction of things not seen."

While we may place hope in our jobs or our future accomplishments or the next season of our lives, our control over these situations is limited. Placing our hope in God assures us that our needs will be met according to His will for our lives, even when life throws us an unexpected twist and even when we can't yet see God's plan playing out in our daily circumstances.

Like the caterpillar hiding in its secret chrysalis, it is a beautiful thing to stay so connected with Jesus that the world doesn't know what's happening. If the caterpillar felt pressure to come out of the chrysalis early and show the world the transformation God was doing, the caterpillar would literally be a soup-like mess and the transformation would stop.

In God's timing, He will display His beautiful works within you, using your life to give Him glory. Every single day, you have to decide that you're going to show up for and with Jesus. Our motivations are no longer the *external* things we can see, but the *eternal* reward we are promised by Him.

You Can't Control the Transformation Process

When I asked my friends to identify the hardest part about doing life with Jesus, they said:

- losing part of myself
- finding the willpower
- staying in a position of surrender
- trying to control what only God can
- letting go of my idea of how my day should go
- letting go of what makes me comfortable
- putting my wants aside
- fear of the unknown
- being caught up with worldly ideas and expectations
- letting go of my ego

When we look at these answers, one theme stands out: control.

Every single day we have to start in a posture of surrender and stay in that position. This reminds me of stretching, more specifically trying to bend over and touch your toes. I remember that I absolutely hated stretching before soccer practice. I knew it was good for me and would protect me from injuries, but I really wanted to skip that part of the process.

Stretching doesn't always feel good, and neither does surrendering. Stretching isn't our natural position or posture, and neither is surrendering. We default to taking things into our hands, trying to maintain control of our lives. When things don't go as expected, we freak out and try to take over what we should be handing over to God.

Similarly to how the caterpillar knew when it was time to leave its old life, you too have been called to spend some time in a secret place. You, like the caterpillar, can't rush this part of the process. All you have to do is stay connected to Jesus, your safe place, and trust that He will transform you, little by little, every day.

We must learn to let go of the expectations we have for the transformation process. It probably isn't going to look like we envisioned, but it will look exactly as God intends.

Can you imagine if a caterpillar knew it was about to become a big, oozy liquid mess? If I were that caterpillar, I would have a freakout moment and probably never go through the process to become what God was calling me to be.

How often do we freak out when life looks different from what we expected? Instead of trying to seize control in those moments, we can learn from the caterpillar and embrace a posture of surrender, trusting that God has placed us exactly where we need to be right NOW in order to prepare us for what comes NEXT.

You Lack Nothing in Jesus

After I got baptized, I went right back to work in my dream job. Even though I had just made the biggest decision of my life, nothing really *felt* different. Advancing with Jesus is not like advancing in the corporate world, where each accomplishment was rewarded with a new title, a new pay raise, or a new recognition. I had left the baptismal with the same title, salary, and external status as I'd had going into the water.

Once again, God was trying to teach me that life with Jesus may not present us with *immediate* changes that the people around us can see.

The best way I can articulate this is by using my marriage with Will as an example. We've been married seven years at the time I'm writing this book. On the outside, I imagine people see us the same way they saw us on June 24, 2017 ... married.

Will and I are the only ones who know how different our marriage is now versus how it was seven years ago. There are things in our marriage that will always be kept private between us and God. Some of those private moments were sweet, and some of those private moments were really hard. Our relationship has grown and continues to grow by doing daily life together. The same is true for our relationship with Jesus.

Think about it.

All the key cells of the butterfly are within the egg from the day the cycle begins, but those parts are hidden from the world. Even as the larva and pupa develop, the world can't see the butterfly forming inside.

Likewise, God is using the giftings and the skills He has given you to develop your life in a whole new way. You have no idea how incredible this transformation is going to be.

Day after day, God showed me that I didn't have to strive to earn His love, His grace, or His acceptance as I had in corporate America. I started to see that He had strategically placed me HERE, NOW, with a very specific purpose—to reflect Him and bring Him glory.

For example, the ministry role I stepped into couldn't have been more perfect for the skill set I had acquired during my climb on the

corporate ladder. But instead of using my gift of charisma to climb higher and higher on that old ladder, He was now using this gift to help me point people to Jesus. Instead of using my go-getter attitude to chase after worldly success, I suddenly wanted to use my energy and drive to make Jesus known to others every single day.

Through God, nothing is wasted. Even when our transformation process looks more like an ooey, gooey mess of a caterpillar, He remains with us, making a way to turn our lives into a beautiful display of His glory.

God will use the skills He put in you from the time you were born. The caterpillar had everything it needed inside of it to become a butterfly, and you have everything you need to transform NOW for what God has NEXT.

> *Even when our transformation process looks more like an ooey, gooey mess of a caterpillar, he remains with us, making a way to turn our lives into a beautiful display of His glory.*

No matter how hard we try, the transformation that prepares us for what is NEXT is not something we can control or hold onto. It's something only God has the blueprint for. Staying connected with Jesus and surrendering our lives to Him is the only way to experience what's to come to the fullest.

We have to trust the opportunities to serve people He has placed around us. We don't have to *see* the impact to believe He is working in us and through us wherever He has placed us.

Just as the caterpillar lacks no parts to become a butterfly, you lack nothing when you remain connected with Jesus. Psalm 23:1–4 says it best:

> The LORD is my shepherd, I lack nothing.
> He makes me lie down in green pastures,
> he leads me beside quiet waters,
> he refreshes my soul.
> He guides me along the right paths for his name's sake.
> Even though I walk
> through the darkest valley,
> I will fear no evil,
> for you are with me;
> your rod and your staff,
> they comfort me. (NIV)

In case you're looking for some ideas on how to get started on giving your life to Jesus daily, here are a few:

- praising and thanking Him
- reading the Bible
- prayer journaling in the mornings
- listening to worship music
- talking to Him throughout the day
- doing the hard things and still having faith

Having a relationship with Jesus used to feel daunting, and I'd put so much pressure on myself. The pressure stifled me to the point

that I didn't know where to start. We learned about the ooey, gooey caterpillar that Jesus looks at and sees a beautiful butterfly within. If He sees a liquid mess of a caterpillar and envisions a butterfly, He sees the beauty in us and who He is transforming us to be through Him.

Perhaps Paul (previously Saul) said it best:

> Here's what I want you to do, God helping you: Take your everyday, ordinary life—your sleeping, eating, going-to-work, and walking-around life— and place it before God as an offering. Embracing what God does for you is the best thing you can do for him. Don't become so well-adjusted to your culture that you fit into it without even thinking. Instead, fix your attention on God. You'll be changed from the inside out. Readily recognize what he wants from you, and quickly respond to it. Unlike the culture around you, always dragging you down to its level of immaturity, God brings the best out of you, develops well-formed maturity in you. (Romans 12:1–2 MSG)

Now that we're ready to make Jesus a part of our everyday lives, it's time for the next phase of our transformation. Turn the page when you're ready.

Embrace the Now

1. Can you identify any specific areas where you may be tempted to take shortcuts? How do these shortcuts impact your relationship with Jesus and what He is doing in your life right now?

2. How can you embrace the slow and unseen process of transformation that God is doing in you, rather than seeking immediate, visible results?

3. How has your perspective started to change on where
God has you now?

4. How can you practice surrender in practical ways,
trusting God's timing and process as He transforms
your life?

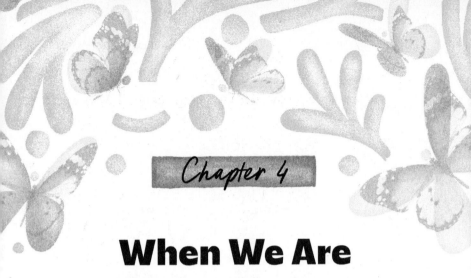

Chapter 4

When We Are Done Making Compromises

When I was in the first grade, I had two best friends, Presley and Kameron. The three of us had a blast together, but one dilemma came up each day during recess. Presley was into playing soccer, and Kameron wanted to play Lizzie McGuire, based on the popular show that every girl loved on the Disney Channel in the 2000s.

Even as a first grader, I struggled with wanting to fit in and please the people around me. Well ... Presley and Kameron both wanted me to play with them. I was terrible at making a decision because I wanted to make both of them happy. I didn't want to miss out, so I got stuck in the middle.

What was their solution? Each of them would grab one of my arms and basically play a game of human tug-of-war with me. Whoever pulled me to their side is who I played with. Some days I

was out in the soccer field with Presley, and other days I was playing Lizzie McGuire with Kameron.

This game of tug-of-war reminds me of how our faith journey often looks. When I was on my corporate ladder, I was living for Jesus, but I also wanted to experience the next best thing that the world had to offer. My values and my actions didn't always align. Like the first-grader Hope, the fear of missing out kept me stuck in the middle. I loved what both the world and Jesus offered me. I wanted the things this world offered *and* the things that Jesus offered.

We have to choose a side.

When we let FOMO control us, we get stuck in the middle and we get comfortable making compromises. I'll give you a few examples from my own life.

During my freshman year of college, I would go to parties because I wanted to experience all that college had to offer. I would tell everyone I wasn't going to drink, but I would wind up taking a sip here and there. I was willing to make a compromise to "fit in." Then, I would end up feeling tipsy from the sum of my tiny compromises throughout the night. I would start feeling lighter and try to convince myself I was simply tired and there was no way I could be tipsy because, remember … I wasn't drinking … I was sipping. My sips made me slip, and the world won on those nights.

Compromises make us feel like we are standing firm in our faith, but they only cover up where the enemy is gaining ground in our lives. When we choose to make a compromise, we adjust a question to fit the answer we want. Compromises may feel small in the moment, but their impact can be large.

"I'll buy it today and pay for it next month when I get the money."

"I didn't say the actual cuss word."

"It's not porn; it's just a movie."

"I couldn't tell her the truth; it would hurt her too much."

The sum of our compromises will only make us more and more comfortable remaining in the middle of this tug-of-war. It keeps us in a cycle that is hard to get out of. It keeps us on a ladder that leads to the next best thing instead of experiencing what God is doing right now.

The goal of this chapter is to step out of the game of tug-of-war and surrender your daily life to the winning side—the side that Jesus is on.

The Side That Requires Compromises Is the Side without Sacrifices

I'll give you another example, although shame from it makes me question if I should really share it. It's not exactly something Christians talk about. But I know I can't be the only one who has struggled with this.

While I was in high school, I was in a relationship that was very controlling. We dated from my sophomore year until the summer before my freshman year of college. One day, I made a physical compromise without really knowing what was happening. Once the compromise happened, I freaked out and I didn't know what to do. Like any compromise, once you start, it's hard to stop.

I didn't want to continue going along with it, but I did. The compromises became more frequent. I feared that if I made a boundary or stood up for what I believed, the relationship would be over. The shame isolated me and made me feel alone. I didn't want to go to God with this because I felt like He was disappointed in me.

I honestly believed that the only way to make my compromises right in the eyes of God was to marry this guy. I thought that once I married him then God would approve of me, and I could go back to His side.

This guy and I were supposed to go to college together. However, eight days before college started, an anonymous donor gave me a full-tuition scholarship to relocate across the country to attend Pepperdine University. This unexpected event changed my college plans.

Compromises may feel small in the moment, but their impact can be large.

As a result, my boyfriend broke up with me, insisting he didn't want to maintain a long-distance relationship. I'll never forget that when I shared my change in plans, his response was, "So, how do you want to take our relationship off Facebook?" That was how our relationship ended.

Yes, I learned the hard way that the side that requires you to make compromises is the side that doesn't love you enough to make sacrifices for you.

I was more upset by the shame that the relationship left me with than the actual breakup. The breakup itself was freeing and something that only God could have gotten me out of. I knew that, but it was hard to see past the shame ... until I met my husband, Will.

There isn't enough time for me to tell you everything I love about Will. Will and I grew up fifteen minutes apart our entire lives, but we didn't meet until we were set up on a blind date our freshman year of college. My sister, Hannah, had known him for a few years, and as soon as she figured out we were both single, she told us we had to meet.

At Hannah's suggestion, we met at a coffee shop and then went to look at Christmas lights. I'll never forget talking to Will and knowing that something about him was different from any other guy I had ever met.

We hung out on New Year's Eve and Will didn't even try to kiss me! I remember thinking, *Who is this guy?* He didn't want something from me; he wanted to be with me ... forever. He wanted what we had to last, even if that meant waiting.

Though we had met during Christmas break, we didn't start officially "dating" until the summer. We only saw each other three times that entire year. I was studying abroad in Switzerland, and Will was playing baseball in Oklahoma, so our entire relationship consisted of three years of long-distance dating until we got married. It's crazy to think about now, but our first time living in the same city was after we got married and were living together in Washington, DC.

Will's love pursues me, fights for me, prioritizes me, and sacrifices for me. His love resembles how God loves us.

God loved us so much that He sent His one and only Son to come to this earth as both fully God and fully human to die for us so that we could spend forever with Him. God chose you. He sacrificed His Son for you. He doesn't want you to have to work for His grace. He freely gives it to you. He doesn't want you to have to do life alone and in your own strength. He doesn't want you to have to sit in your sin or your shortcomings. He wants to rescue you and pull you over to the winning side today. He wants to do life with you NOW.

On the other side of this tug-of-war match, the enemy, or Satan, is doing everything he can to make this world look appealing. He is showing you everything he can to gain ground in your life, not because he loves you but because he wants you to suffer with him. He has already lost. He knows the plans and purpose God has for you, and he wants to stop you from stepping into who you were created to be.

He wants you to be comfortable living in the middle and never experiencing what God has for you now. He wants to dangle worldly rewards in front of you, distracting you so you don't see what God is doing today. He wants you to compromise, to slip. He wants to take you away from Jesus. He hasn't given up a thing for you.

Even though the enemy would love for you to think that this game of tug-of-war is as innocent as the game I played with Presley and Kameron, it isn't. The stakes are as high as they get.

Play to Win

Playing to win this match of tug-of-war requires us to surrender our strength and give our life to Jesus every single day. Doing life with Jesus produces humility, not pride.

The old, striving Hope had let the world win. I didn't want to admit I wasn't perfect. I was full of pride. I didn't want to miss out on people seeing me as the girl who had it all together. I didn't want to miss out on the next best thing the world had to offer. I thought I was living for Jesus, but now I can see I was living for myself, still taking tiny "sips" to conform, as I let the enemy tug me toward the American Dream.

First Peter 2:9–10 says, "But you are the ones chosen by God, chosen for the high calling of priestly work, chosen to be a holy people, God's instruments to do his work and speak out for him, to tell others of the night-and-day difference he made for you—from nothing to something, from rejected to accepted" (MSG).

When we decide we aren't going to keep letting FOMO dictate how we live, we have to surrender our lives to Jesus. When we decide there is more to life than how we've been living, we have to surrender our lives to Jesus. Surrendering is where real transformation takes place.

Surrendering our daily lives to Jesus is the result of shifting our hope from the seen to the unseen. Surrendering activates our faith and lights a fire in our soul. It takes us from dead to alive. It's where we get the courage and the boldness to trust Him and give up on trying to take life into our own hands. It's where God proves His goodness and His kindness and reminds us of His promises. It's where God shows up in the most unexpected and exciting ways.

While the caterpillar is inside its chrysalis, it is being prepared to come out living in an entirely new way. It has to surrender daily to the plan God has for it. It doesn't yet know what's ahead, but everything about it is being transformed.

It's in the chrysalis that the caterpillar goes from:

- feeding on solid milkweed to drinking a
  liquid diet
- no wings to functional wings
- stubby legs to long legs
- poor eyesight to good vision
- growing to reproducing

If there wasn't proof that a caterpillar changed into a butterfly, I probably wouldn't believe that a little worm-looking bug could possibly turn into something so beautiful.

I share this to say … get ready for your life to look and feel different.

Striving is a way of living with pride, while surrendering is a way of living with humility. The world produces pride, while Jesus produces humility.

It may look like nothing is going on inside the chrysalis, but big changes are happening. There are big changes happening inside you right now too.

When we choose to surrender our plans, dreams, and expectations to Jesus, He transforms us. He makes us new! Like the caterpillar, beautiful changes aren't only coming our way; they are happening right NOW.

We're shifting from:

- finding fulfillment in worldly things to filling ourselves
  up with Jesus

- striving and feeling like the pressure is all on us (pride) to knowing that God's grace is a gift, not something we have to earn (humility)
- pleasing the people around us to pleasing God
- placing our hope in things that are seen to placing our hope in the unseen
- focusing our eyes on the next best thing around the corner to focusing our eyes on Jesus
- serving ourselves to serving those around us

If the caterpillar didn't surrender to the transformation that only God could make happen inside the chrysalis, it would never become a butterfly. If we are ever to become our fullest selves, we have to surrender to God's plan for us.

Striving is a way of living with pride, while surrendering is a way of living with humility. The world produces pride, while Jesus produces humility.

It's in the daily surrender that we witness the impossible, the unseen, the unexplainable, the MIRACLES.

I used to be scared of change. I wanted to plan everything far into my future, assuring myself I was doing everything in my power to create the best life imaginable. But now I know that letting go and surrendering is the only way to step into what God is doing NOW.

God Restores Us and Makes Us New

We see the same thing in Jacob's story in the Bible. Here are a few key things Jacob did to try to step into what God promised him next:

- He deceived his father, Isaac, by pretending to be his brother, Esau.
- He tricked Esau into giving up his birthright for a bowl of stew.
- He manipulated his father-in-law, Laban, by playing games with livestock deals.
- He became entangled in schemes that made his own brother want to kill him.

After Jacob heard from God in a dream and received special promises, he *still* wrestled with God. Even though the Bible tells us the promises God gives us, we *still* wrestle. Wrestling or playing tug-of-war isn't a new thing. FOMO isn't new either.

When we look at Jacob's life, we see him trying to take matters into his own hands. He struggled with FOMO, as we do today. I used to think the fear of missing out was helping us see gaps in our lives so we could fill them, but now I see that the fear of missing out points out gaps in our lives that only God can fill.

Jacob's humanness often came out, and so did the humanness of those around him. He hurt others and others hurt him. Jacob's story reminds us of the messiness that comes when we try to control our lives. But in the middle of Jacob's chaos, there's a beautiful

moment—a wrestling match between him and God that leads to transformation and restoration.

In Genesis 32, Jacob decided to visit his brother, Esau. This meet and greet was no small thing. In fact, it could have meant his life was over. (Remember how his brother wanted to kill him?) When Jacob was approaching Esau, fear got the best of him. He sent his entire family ahead of him. And when he was all alone, he wrestled with God (vv. 22–29).

Jacob was desperate for some kind of sign or blessing, and he wanted it NOW!

God met him in the struggle, and He meets us in our struggle. After the "wrestling match," Jacob proceeded to meet his brother, as planned. But while Jacob had feared Esau would kill him, Genesis 33:4 shows how God had better plans in store for these brothers: "Esau ran to meet Jacob and embraced him; he threw his arms around his neck and kissed him. And they wept" (NIV).

You know what else God did for Jacob? He told him that he would no longer be called Jacob and would now be called Israel (32:28). Just as Saul became Paul, Jacob transformed into the best version of himself *only* after he had endured the worst form of himself. Just like the butterfly emerges from a chrysalis of soup!

God's response to Jacob's wrestling gives a sneak peek into what is waiting on the other side of our game of tug-of-war right now. By surrendering to Jesus and placing our faith in God's plan, we will emerge from this season with a new identity, a new hope, and a new future. God stands ready to make all things new right NOW. All we have to do is surrender to Him.

You Don't Have to Do It in Your Own Strength

The incredible thing about tug-of-war is that Jesus is not only pulling for us, but He also offers us His strength. It doesn't matter what weakness FOMO has created in our life; His strength is enough. We learn in 2 Corinthians 12:7–8 that Paul had some type of handicap. Whatever it was, he tells us it kept him from being filled with pride.

He even asked for Jesus to take it away from him. In verse 9, we see both Jesus' response to Paul asking him to take it away and Paul's change in perspective: "He said to me, 'My grace is sufficient for you, for my power is made perfect in weakness.' Therefore I will boast all the more gladly about my weaknesses, so that Christ's power may rest on me" (NIV).

When we surrender our lives to Jesus, our weaknesses and shortcomings become a story that screams God's goodness and restoration. Think about the redemption story He wrote through my marriage and my career. He will do the same for you.

It's in the tug-of-war that your testimony is being written. It's in the tug-of-war that you're reminded of your weakness and how desperately you need Jesus. Day by day, your life and the story God is writing will become more and more beautiful. The butterfly in you is developed through saying things like this every single day:

- I didn't want this for my life, but I trust you, God.
- I don't know how this is for Your glory, but give me
  Your strength to walk through this.
- I really wanted something else to happen, but I know
  You have better plans for me.

- I loved what You are leading me away from, but I love You more.
- I wish I knew what was coming next, but I know that all I have to focus on is what You're doing now.
- I don't see what You're doing, but I choose to believe that You're alive and moving in my life.
- I wouldn't have put myself in this situation or place, but I know You have a purpose for me today.
- I don't know how much longer You're going to have me here, but I trust Your perfect timing.

Changes in Your Heart's Desires

God began placing an unexpected desire in my heart several months into working in my dream job. How? I was feeling called to press Pause on my career completely so I could focus on caring for Remi full-time. As you know, I loved working, so this was very odd.

Before I share where God led me next, I want to make one thing clear: we all have different callings on our lives in the kingdom of God. In fact, depending on different seasons of our lives, we need to be open to where we are being called to serve Him. The mission field He has for you might be within the walls of corporate America or serving in your church or starting a personal business, founding a nonprofit, becoming a stay-at-home mom, or being a caregiver … and the list goes on. There is no right or wrong answer here; it's where the Lord reveals He is calling you to.

I was so grateful God had led me to this ministry role and blessed our family with a wonderful daycare for Remi that had brought us

peace. I was thankful God had gotten me through my breakdown and that He had begun healing me. Now, I was praying that He would catch me as I considered taking another leap of faith.

Will and I both wanted this shift for our family, but as we crunched the numbers in our Excel budget sheet, we couldn't make the math work. Without my income, we would be short every single month. Our lifestyle was going to have to change … again. This time we'd likely need to sell our home. And even then, I wasn't sure the numbers were adding up.

FOMO wanted me to stay stuck in the middle of tug-of-war. FOMO was quick to remind me that surrendering my income would make my little family of three miss out on too many things we needed in life.

> When we surrender our lives to Jesus, our weaknesses and shortcomings become a story that screams God's goodness and restoration.

Ironically, God's will for our lives is always better than what we could or would have planned for ourselves. If God was leading me to be a full-time stay-at-home mother, then He would make a way for us, even if our monthly expenses were making us believe it was impossible.

Once again, I turned to Paul's teachings in 2 Corinthians 4:16–18 to encourage me:

> So we're not giving up. How could we! Even though on the outside it often looks like things are falling apart on us, on the inside, where God is making new life, not a day goes by without his unfolding grace. These hard times are small potatoes compared to the coming good times, the lavish celebration prepared for us. There's far more here than meets the eye. The things we see now are here today, gone tomorrow. But the things we can't see now will last forever. (MSG)

I prayed:

> *Lord, the seen has nothing on the unseen. If this desire to stay at home and take care of Remi isn't from You, then please take it away. Seasons shift, but You are steady. Lord, I'll stay still as You fight for me. I surrender it all to You, Lord. If it is Your will, please provide a way for me to stay home with Remi.*

When you surrender to God's will, be prepared to emerge with new wings. Because even when we can't see evidence of it, big things are happening!

Embrace the Now

1. In what ways have you experienced a tug-of-war
between your faith and the world?

2. How have you made compromises in your values or
beliefs in the past to fit in or gain approval?

3. Can you think of a moment when a mistake or failure
led to a lesson or turning point in your life? How did
God use it for His good and His glory? If you can't

see His goodness in it yet, that's okay—it just means
He isn't done!

4. Are you struggling to know what to do next or what
God is calling you to? If yes, what is it? How can you
give this to God?

5. Use this space to write out a prayer. Surrender your
situation over to God and ask Him to fulfill His will
with your life.

Chapter 5

When Our Prayers Aren't Answered How We Expected

Sometimes we go to God like we would go to a doctor. We go to Him in prayer with a remedy in mind. We think we know what we are struggling with and what prescription would ease the suffering. We want a quick fix.

This is the part of the book where I have more questions than answers. I truly do not know why:

- the Christian life is a life full of suffering
- sin had to enter the world
- Satan had to turn against God
- we experience hard times
- we get stuck in the middle of situations that we couldn't make up if we tried

- life can feel so lonely
- stepping into what God has for us requires us to make sacrifices
- it feels like God doesn't hear our prayers
- God can't tell us exactly what we are supposed to be doing in an audible voice
- tragic, terrible things happen

Like going to the doctor with a specific outcome in mind, how often do we go to God with an agenda, hoping He will give us what we think we need to solve our problem?

When I went to God about my desire to stay home with Remi, I had a prescription in mind. I wanted Him to answer these prayers in a way that wouldn't require our family to have to walk through difficult decisions or hard times. I had pictured that God would open doors for Will to make more money and then we'd make the decision that it was time for me to be obedient to what God had placed on my heart.

God often answers our prayers in unexpected ways and through situations we wouldn't have chosen for ourselves.

I'll tell you the hard news first. You're going to have to continue walking with Jesus and trusting what God is doing. Even when you haven't seen any signs of improvement or changes, you have to keep going and give your life to Him every single day. I can't promise you that things will get better or easier, but I can promise you that God's goodness will shine through this situation.

The good news is we get to continue walking with Jesus, the one who understands what it is like to be a human on this earth. I don't

find it a coincidence that the Bible reveals to us a time when God didn't answer Jesus' prayer the way He wanted. When it was almost time for Jesus to die on the cross for us, He told God: "Father, if you are willing, take this cup from me; yet not my will, but yours be done" (Luke 22:42 NIV).

We can see here that Jesus wasn't jumping up and down begging to experience a brutal crucifixion and face all the suffering that was ahead of Him, but He was willing to be obedient to whatever God's will was for Him, even though He had done nothing to deserve the death penalty. Jesus knew that God knew best.

Our Suffering Allows Us to Make Jesus SEEN and KNOWN

Remember what happened after Jesus died? The sun stopped shining from noon to three o'clock in the afternoon (Luke 23:44). It looked like the people who wanted Him dead had won. God didn't immediately reveal how He was going to use this terrible, indescribable situation for His good.

Jesus laid to rest in His tomb for three days. Only THEN did Jesus rise from the dead. Only in God's perfect timing.

When Jesus went to visit the disciples, they thought they were seeing a ghost (24:37). He let them touch Him as proof that He was risen! Right after this, they ate together, and Jesus told His disciples they were being called as witnesses to the promises God was fulfilling through Him now (vv. 46–48).

I think today we feel all this pressure to have the answers. What if we have gotten our role wrong?

When I see what God is doing in the lives of other Christians and I can't see what He is doing in my life, I struggle with FOMO. To put it in simpler terms, I've struggled with my role most when I'm looking at myself in comparison with everyone else around me.

For example, I have seen Christian influencers gain large followings online. I have really wrestled with FOMO as my worldly desires led me to want to be more like THEM. When selfishness got the best of me, I would turn to my prayer journal and speak truth to Jesus:

> *Lord, You have blessed me in so many ways, and I know I lack nothing, but I am struggling with negative thoughts: my book sucks, no one wants to follow me, my nonprofit isn't going to get off of the ground, and I'll never get another book deal. I see these other people with access to money and a growing following. It feels like You are calling me to do these things and not giving me the resources I need to do them. What is Your will for my life? Forgive me of my selfishness and sin, please.*

I love how Jesus uses the word *witness* when He tells the disciples what they are supposed to do with everything they saw God do through Him. I believe that our role right here, right now, is to be a witness. We aren't called to be the one who is seen. We are called to tell the world what we have *seen* God do in our lives. We aren't called to be the one who is known. We are called to use our whole lives to make Him *known*.

Our Best Solution Has Nothing on God's Best for Us

Early one morning, Remi started stirring in her crib and I knew she was hungry.

I woke up, made her a bottle, and then went to feed her. When I picked her up out of her crib, I took away her pacifier and she screamed. Just as we don't expect God to lead us to a place of suffering, Remi didn't expect me to take away her pacifier.

It was dark, and she couldn't see the bottle I had prepared for her. She thought I had taken away her "best" solution, but what she didn't know was that I had something so much better in store for her. I had prepared food that would fulfill her in a way the pacifier could never sustain her.

This is some tough love, but there will be times during our transformation when we want to scream like Remi. We are going to find ourselves in a place where the very thing we depended on as our "best" solution is taken away from us and we will have no idea how we're going to manage life without it. Time and time again, I quit doing something that is good for me because I'm not seeing progress, change, or transformation fast enough. I'm quick to go all in, and I'm quick to burn out.

My fitness goals are the perfect example. Over and over again, I'll decide I want to get back in shape. Then I'll go on a run only to become discouraged when the workout proves challenging. Instead of continuing to take my workouts slowly, I quit when the pain becomes too much. And still, I'll complain that I'm not in shape.

Sound familiar? Whether it's a physical workout or a spiritual one, we can't rush the process. We have to move at the pace God intends for us.

Our Suffering and Sacrifices Give God Glory

Let me tell you about how I have witnessed God's goodness, faithfulness, provision, and restoration in my own life through suffering, trials, and unexpected answers to my prayers. Nine months into working in my dream job, the very thing that Will and I saw as our little family of three's "best" solution was ripped away from us.

It started when our extended family members were considering opening a daycare in the area. The owners of Remi's daycare were not happy about this potential competition. Even though we were not involved in the business plans in any way, they were now using a one-year-old—*our one-year-old*—as a symbol of protest for someone else's corporate decision.

They quickly let us know that they would no longer be willing to care for Remi. They didn't want us coming in and out of their day-care facility anymore. This was one of those moments that I sat there and asked myself, *Is this really happening right now?*

I looked at the couple and said, "This is going to impact our family. Without daycare, I will have to quit my job. Without my income, we may have to sell our house."

Before I had become a mom, people had made me feel like the last resort for my baby should be daycare. I had wrestled with the reality of being a working mom so much during my pregnancy. I'd

tried to do everything I possibly could to keep Remi from having to go to daycare.

When we resorted to sending Remi to daycare, we were careful to choose the best option for our family. When she'd aged out of the infant classroom, her teachers gave me a book filled with notes that called out the gifts and potential they could see in her. They noted her sensitive spirit, her determination, and her ability to accomplish any challenge in front of her. We felt so blessed by her teachers, grateful that God had been so faithful to provide our Remi with incredible caregivers who we'd all grown to love and consider family. Without their love, care, and support, I wouldn't have been able to do everything God was calling me to do.

> *It is in our suffering that He calls us to place Him and His will above everything else in our life.*

Now I was learning that just because something is God's will for one season doesn't mean it is God's will for the next season. When our circumstances and trials want to "stick it to us," God will use those same pain points to save us.

But I couldn't yet see God at work in that daycare meeting. Instead, I started crying at the table. I was seconds away from asking Will to meet me outside when the meeting was over, but I decided to shift my perspective. Instead of walking out the door, I walked to the

restroom, took a few minutes to get myself together again, and went right back to the conversation with confidence.

God doesn't take away our best without giving us something better, and I wasn't going to let this situation get the best of me.

God was doing something here. Was this happening the way I'd expected? No, but I didn't want to miss what He was doing. And I don't want you to miss what He's doing in your life either.

As my nana said in chapter 1, "FOMO could make us miss a blessing." More often than not, the answers to our prayers look like dead ends, and they require us to lose something.

It is in our suffering that He calls us to place Him and His will above everything else in our lives. It is in our suffering that He shows us that the way our situation looks is much different from how it is going to turn out. Through the hard times, we get to experience God in a way that our comfortable, prescriptive prayers would never allow us to step into.

I may not have a "prescription" or answers for you in this chapter. All we can do is learn to look at our situation, no matter how hopeless it may seem, and be a witness to how God wants us to focus on NOW over NEXT.

Jesus Fills Us Up

We can once again see parallels in our transformation and a butterfly's. I can't be the only one who pictured a butterfly emerging out of its chrysalis and immediately fluttering away to show off its new wings to the world. In reality, a butterfly breaks out of its chrysalis with crumpled, wet wings and a belly full of fluid.

The butterfly doesn't immediately fly away. First, it must spend time hanging upside down on the chrysalis. This allows the fluid in its belly to expand its wings. Once its wings have expanded, the butterfly then waits until its wings are dry before it takes its first flight.

Like the butterfly, we can only cross over into the NEXT if we look at our life through the lens that God's upside-down kingdom reveals to us. Just as the butterfly stays connected to the chrysalis when it first emerges, we can't cross over into the NEXT and find our new way of living without staying connected to the Way Maker in the NOW.

If a butterfly doesn't have room to hang upside down on its chrysalis, it will have deformed wings for the rest of its life and it'll never be able to fully cross over into its new life. The same is true for us. If we don't make space for Jesus NOW, we won't ever cross over into the NEXT thing He wants to do in and through us. We can't be filled up by Jesus if we aren't connected to Him.

Again, let's remember what Jesus tells us in John 15:4: "Live in me. Make your home in me just as I do in you. In the same way that a branch can't bear grapes by itself but only by being joined to the vine, you can't bear fruit unless you are joined with me" (MSG).

If you had told me that in 2024 I would be stepping away from the career where I had found my security, worth, and identity, I wouldn't have believed you. Jesus is the only explanation I have for how this *new Hope* is here today. The same is true for the new you too. Jesus is the only way we can expand our "wings" and "fly" to the places God has planned for us.

Less of Us Means More Room for Jesus

With the daycare no longer an option for Remi, God had made it clear that I really was supposed to step away from my career and become a full-time mother. But how could I tell my team that I was stepping away?

I could have called them, but instead I decided to tell them in person. This required that I travel to Oklahoma City, a three-and-a-half-hour drive from my house. The closer I got to the office, the more the reality of this decision set in. Was I really going to leave the job I loved? The job God had called me to when the corporate ladder had become too much?

Once again, I was full of FOMO, but I trusted that Jesus loved me and had something even better in store on the other side of this resignation.

I told my teammates about my decision in the same conference room where I had first been interviewed for the position nine months earlier. I even sat in the middle seat on the right side of the table—the same spot I'd chosen for my interview. Bittersweet tears flooded my eyes when each teammate asked how I was doing. With complete peace, I was able to say that I was ready for what God was up to, even if I couldn't yet see what that might be.

Even after I put in my resignation, Will and I weren't sure how we were going to pull this off from a financial perspective. The first thing to let go of was my car. We'd purchased this car shortly after I'd started working in my dream ministry role. It was the "mom car" I had always pictured myself driving kids around in, another symbol of pride, success, and accomplishment. Now, we were in a spot where this token of my "dream life" looked more like excess.

The easiest way to reduce our expenses was to list the vehicle on Facebook Marketplace. Within twenty-four hours of listing it, the car sold. It was all happening so fast! Now we would be sharing one vehicle as we moved into this new way of living.

God used our vehicle (something we already had) to transport us into this new season for our family. The world would say, "Keep your car. You have to have a way to get around." The things we think can move us ahead in life have nothing on how God can MOVE in our lives and where He can take us when we give our entire lives to Him. Less of us means only one thing: more of Jesus.

Will and I spent the next few weeks discussing and praying about how to prioritize our family's needs and adjust our budget to fit within his salary. This required making some major shifts, including selling anything we didn't really need. One day, I had forgotten how much we'd put up for sale. A friend called me and said, "I've seen you put up your blender, your car, and other things that filled your house. I want you to know that I see all that you're giving up right now, and I want you to know how proud I am of you."

> Less of us means only one thing: more of Jesus.

I can't really explain how it felt to let go of all those things that had once filled our lives. While it may seem as if it would have been sad to let go of all the material things we had worked so hard to acquire, it was actually ... freeing! All those things that had once

filled me with happiness had nothing on the joy that came from being filled with Jesus.

The things of this world are meaningless. Jesus means everything. If you have Jesus, you aren't lacking a thing. This is coming from a twenty-nine-year-old mom without a job who is sharing a truck with her husband. I have fewer "things" than I've had in years, and yet my life is *fuller* than ever.

It is only in the suffering, sacrifice, and surrender that we experience His provision, abundance, blessings, goodness, faithfulness, and restoration.

Embrace the Now

1. Reflect on a time when you approached God with a specific solution in mind. How did the outcome differ from your expectations, and what did God teach you through this? How was His plan compared to your plans?

2. How have times of suffering in your life strengthened your faith? What is a verse you can cling to when you are going through hard times?

3. Think about a prayer that went unanswered or was
answered differently than how you expected. How did
this shape your understanding of God's will and timing
in your life?

4. What do you want to be freed from today? What strongholds are in your life? How can you let go of those and
surrender them to God?

Chapter 6

When We Step into Something New

When my sister, Hannah, and I were little kids, we always talked our parents into getting new pets. Throughout our childhood, we had hamsters, frogs, fish, guinea pigs, cats, dogs, turtles, hermit crabs, ants, butterflies, and even a baby squirrel. I have some memories of each of the animals, but I remember almost every detail about the butterflies. I can remember being so excited for the caterpillars to come in the mail and running to the mailbox with Hannah every day to check if they had arrived.

When we got our caterpillars, we watched them for hours each day. We couldn't believe they would turn into butterflies. The transformation was mesmerizing to us. Our mom had briefed us on what was going to happen, but we never could have prepared ourselves for the day we walked in to check on them and saw butterflies!

We squealed and ran to get Mom. When we went back to show her, I expected to find them flying around the pop-up habitat we had kept them in. Instead, they were … climbing.

The butterflies looked different, but they didn't yet know what to do with their new wings. Out of habit, they had gone right back to operating like they had when they were caterpillars.

When we watched closely, we were able to see that they were trying to test out their new wings. They would stop climbing for a second and flutter their wings, as if they were thinking, *Whoa! What are these new things?! Let me stop for a second to figure out how to use this new thing I have.*

Like butterflies, our transformation takes time.

Climbing in the New

Right before I quit my dream job, Will told me he had one concern. He worried that I would find other ways to work that would possibly distract me from being fully present in my new role as a full-time mom to Remi. At first, I was offended. I couldn't believe he would even think such a thing. I remember feeling so hurt and telling him how unfair it was for him to have this thought.

Well … Will knows me better than anyone else.

As he'd predicted, I stepped into this new role and, like the freshly emerged butterfly, I operated the way I had always done. I shot out of the gate like I was off to get a promotion. I lined up playdates like I was establishing meetings with key stakeholders. I scheduled Remi's naptime full of meetings that would help me reach the new goals I wanted to accomplish. I had never had a couple hours in the middle of

the day to do whatever I wanted, so I planned to use every minute to strategically grow my online ministry.

On top of this, I wanted to use this time to be the wife I'd always wanted to be. I wanted to try out new recipes and have an incredible dinner waiting for Will with the table set when he walked in the door from work each day. I wanted our home to be spotless and squeaky clean. I didn't want Will to have to walk our goldendoodle, Sadie, after work, so I planned to take her with Remi during the day. The laundry was going to get done, and the clothes would be folded and put away each day.

I was going to exceed Will's expectations. I created a project plan with timelines I needed to hit, just as I'd done in my career. On Sundays, I would find new recipes to try out for the week and get groceries. I knew what time I needed to start cooking dinner each day. I cleaned on Tuesdays. I started a load of laundry every morning. And the list goes on.

It didn't take a week to feel burned out. Remi's routine wasn't as routine as I'd thought it was going to be. I got frustrated when she didn't nap during the time I'd planned because, remember … I had meetings that were going to push my desires for this season forward. The laundry looked like a mountain. By the time it was dinner, Remi would cry until I'd pick her up because she wanted the attention I hadn't given her that day. Will would come home, and I'd tell him we needed to go out to eat. The house was a wreck. Toys covered the floor in our living room, and Will started doing the household chores … before and after work.

I was struggling with this transition, and so was Remi. I started fixating on all the people around me who had what I wanted … free

time to do what they wanted. I started feeling bad for myself, and this new thing didn't feel fun and exciting anymore.

> *The enemy wants us to miss out on God's plan for us because he knows how impactful and powerful our stepping into this new thing is going to be.*

Once again, I was allowing FOMO to drive my decisions. It is ironic because I didn't want to miss out on an opportunity to grow my ministry, but I was missing out on my greatest ministry right in front of me—Remi and Will. I share the ugly parts of my heart here in hopes that this helps you spot the sneaky ways the enemy might be trying to stop you too.

Where has God placed you right now?
What are you trying to climb toward right now?

The enemy used something I thought was good—my desire to tell more people about Jesus—to distract me from the new thing God stood ready to do for me. During this time, I became obsessed with posting on social media and finding opportunities to speak to women. The enemy makes it so hard to see that something good you've set out to do is really about *you*. And, come on. Who really wants to admit that something you are saying that you're doing for Jesus and Him alone isn't 100 percent about Jesus?

The enemy wants us to miss out on God's plan for us because he knows how impactful and powerful our stepping into this new thing is going to be.

I decided to go to Will and be honest with how I was struggling with this new role. Of course, Will knew this already. Jesus knew this too. Even though my husband had predicted that this would happen from the beginning, he responded with love and grace. He didn't say he'd told me so … like he could have. Instead, he sat down and talked it through with me. He asked me how I was feeling, what I was struggling with, and what I wanted to do about it.

At the end, he said, "All I expect from you right now is to take care of Remi."

Will wanted me to do the one thing I was being called to in this season—take care of Remi. All the pressure was from myself.

I wanted to be a good wife and mother, but I was feeling tired, overwhelmed, and confused. FOMO was still driving me to compare and compete with others in the world. I prayed for God to please help me to be content in my new role as a stay-at-home mom. I determined that if it was His will to use me here in our home, then that alone would be *more* than enough and *more* than I deserved.

What expectations are you carrying into your new season?
What new season is God asking you to step into NOW?

We don't make it easy on God, do we? We want the new thing, but we also want the comfort of our old thing. We want the healing, but we also want minimal pain in the process. We want soul-deep

joy, but we also want to be "happy." We want God's will, but we also want worldly success.

When Remi first started walking, she still preferred to crawl. She wasn't very strong, and she fell often. She didn't want to experience the pain that came with her new ability to walk, so she would go back to what she knew.

How true is this for us?

This new thing God is doing requires us to operate in a new way, even if it's scary, hard, or painful at first. Imagine if Remi had kept crawling, never trusting her God-given abilities to move through the world in this new way. Just as the butterfly eventually learns to fly and children eventually learn to walk, God will call us to our new season in the right time. All we have to do is answer the call.

Do You Want to Get Well?

This transformational journey we're moving through reminds me of a story in John 5 about Jesus healing a man who couldn't walk. Jesus traveled to a pool in Jerusalem where many people with disabilities had gathered (vv. 2–3). People believed that when this pool bubbled, the first person to jump into the waters would be healed.

Jesus *saw* the lame man and *knew* he had been in this state for thirty-eight years and had been waiting for healing for a long time. He didn't go up to the man and immediately give him healing. Instead, He asked him the question: "Do you want to get well?" (vv. 5–6 MSG).

Why would Jesus ask this man a question with such an obvious answer? Clearly, the man wanted healing. Otherwise, he wouldn't have been waiting at the pool.

I think Jesus asked him this because He wanted the man to check his heart. I think Jesus wanted him to examine what he was thinking and how he was living. I think Jesus wanted this man to decide if he really wanted everything that came with healing.

Do you want to get well?

Jesus knew that true healing comes with new responsibilities. If this man really wanted healing, he was no longer going to be disabled. He was going to be able to walk. He was going to have new responsibilities. He was going to have to work.

> *Just as the butterfly eventually learns to fly and children eventually learn to walk, God will call us to our new season in the right time.*

Jesus wants healing for us, but He doesn't force it on us.

Do you really want everything that is going to come with this new thing God is doing now?

Look at how the man first responded to Jesus: "'Sir,' the invalid replied, 'I have no one to help me into the pool when the water is stirred. While I am trying to get in, someone else goes down ahead of me'" (v. 7 NIV).

This man sounds a lot like me. I was walking in an answered prayer, but I was stuck in my expectations. This man had an idea of *how* his healing was going to happen. He had sat there waiting for a

long time for someone to help him get into the pool so he could experience healing.

I'm not proud of this, but I secretly saw staying home with Remi as an opportunity to advance my own goals and desires. I hadn't only wanted to be a full-time mother. I also wanted to be a full-time author, speaker, podcaster, and nonprofit founder ... and I believed that staying home with Remi would give me the time to accomplish those things too. I wanted to grow my ministry and step into big, exciting, and lucrative opportunities like the other Christian influencers I admired (and envied).

Jesus wanted more for me, and He wants more for you too. When He asked the man if he wanted to be well, Jesus was ultimately asking if the man truly wanted to experience all that God had in store for him.

This man, like us, was so stuck in what *had been the case* that he wasn't able to see WHO was right in front of him: Jesus.

How often do we, like this man, not see Jesus right in front of us? How often do we, like this man, want everything Jesus has to offer, but also want the new season to play out a certain way?

Guess how Jesus responded to this man's excuses. He said, "Get up!" (v. 8 NIV). Jesus didn't sit down next to him and give him a hug and justify how he felt. Jesus didn't help the man enter the water so he could be healed. Instead, Jesus simply called on the man to take action. He instructed the man to GET UP and embrace the new NOW that Jesus was offering him.

Do you hear what Jesus is telling us? It is time to GET UP! Everything that comes with being well is *right in front of us*. Right NOW. His name is Jesus!

Get Up

I want to tell you about my mother-in-law, Janis. When her friends are sick, she doesn't ask them if she can bring them dinner. Instead, she brings them dinner. She doesn't wait until someone asks her for help; she simply steps up and helps. She doesn't try to figure out ways around the hard stuff; she rolls up her sleeves and figures out how to get it done. She is often behind the scenes and never strives to be front and center. She is happy to be used by God anywhere He has her.

To give you a more personal example, she broke her collarbone the week Remi was born, but she continued helping us as if nothing had happened. There were times I forgot she was hurt! She isn't someone who lets excuses stop her. On the days when I was struggling with my new norm, I would remind myself of how Janis lives her life.

I really wanted to be well. I really wanted everything that came with the new season Jesus was offering me.

And I know you do too.

Maybe "getting up" looks like waking up to what is right in front of us: Jesus.

To do this, we have to ask some deep questions and face some tough truths. The enemy does sneaky things when we step into a new season. He will do anything he can to pull us back over to his side. He doesn't play fair.

These are some questions we can ask ourselves today:

- How are we used to operating?
- What behaviors come with the old us?
- How can we put a stop to these old ways of living when they pop back up in this new season?

- Do we have any selfish desires in this new season?
- How can we hand over our selfish motives to Jesus daily?
- What excuses keep us stuck in old patterns of behavior?
- What is stopping us from seeing Jesus right in front of us?
- What from our past can we not seem to let go of?
- What shame do we carry?
- What makes us feel unqualified or insecure?

These are hard questions, and the answers might surprise you— similar to how I didn't understand why Will would think that I would show up in this new role the same way I had done in my past roles—but the answers don't surprise Jesus.

In the same way that Jesus saw and knew the lame man, Jesus *sees* and *knows* you.

If Jesus didn't spend time sitting with the lame man in the excuses he shared, we don't need to spend time dwelling on excuses either. Share your heart with Jesus. Tell Him the honest truth. Make time and space to really sit with Him in prayer. Ask that He reveal to you the truth you need.

Let's get up and go to Him together now:

Dear God,

We all know there is more to life than the way we have been living. We've been focused on NEXT

when You want us to see the blessings You're giving us NOW. But changing our old ways will cost
us something. We know that following Jesus has a
cost, but, Lord, this is hard.

Can You please give us the strength to trust
that You have us right where You want us NOW?
Will You please reveal to us what is keeping us striving, comparing, and competing? Can You empower
us to conquer FOMO and see that You have blessed
us in ways we never noticed?

Show us the parts of ourselves that we've
wanted to avoid and have felt shameful about. Use
every single part of our lives for Your glory. Lord,
we want Jesus and everything that comes with
accepting Him as our Savior.

We want to be well. Help us to experience Your
grace in a way that we haven't before. We want Your
healing even if that transition proves painful. We
want our lives to look more and more like Jesus
every day. It is worth the cost. It is worth dying to
ourselves to live a life that gives You glory. We want
to reflect You, God.

Please forgive us where we have fallen short and
put ourselves at the center. Holy Spirit, convict us
where we need to be convicted even if it's hard. Use
everything You reveal to us through Your Spirit to
make us new, Lord. In Jesus' name we pray, amen!

Embrace the Now

1. Reflect on a time when you entered a new season of life. How did you navigate the transition, and what challenges did you face in letting go of your old way of living?

2. What expectations are you carrying right now?

3. How can you focus your eyes on what God has called you to now?

4. What are some ways you can remain present and show up where you are?

5. Jesus asked the lame man, "Do you want to get well?" Reflect on your life and identify areas where you might be resistant to change or healing. What steps can you take to embrace the new thing Jesus is offering you now?

Chapter 7

When We Live with Nothing to Fear

I love taking showers at night. There is something about letting the water wash away everything that came with the day. I use this time to get deep into my thoughts. I talk to God about the good, the bad, and the in-between.

One night I found myself in the shower feeling sorry for myself. I was standing there watching Remi's monitor on my phone and feeling depleted. I felt helpless and I had nothing left to give. I felt all alone and unseen. I felt doomed.

In my past life, when I'd had a career of my own, my hard work was rewarded with acknowledgments and external praise. But here, at home, I was not recognized for my hard work. Only God knew everything I had done throughout the day, and I really wanted to give up.

I missed being surrounded by people who could talk all day. I missed seeing fast progress and results in my life. I missed climbing. I missed control. I missed the old Hope.

Who was this new Hope? She felt like a stranger. She felt unqualified. She missed the corporate life, and she longed to go back to the success the world had offered. She wanted a sense of control again. She didn't like playing a "small role."

I found myself frustrated with God because our extended family members had decided not to open the daycare after all. Had all of this been for nothing? Was I wrong to have stepped away from my high-paying corporate career? Was I wrong to have stepped away from the dream job I'd loved? All these changes had impacted us financially. I no longer had the freedom to buy whatever I wanted or to splurge on the little things anymore.

I felt like I had been constantly giving things up for Him, and all I had gotten in return was more suffering. I felt like there was nothing left of me. I was having an identity crisis.

As the warm water hit my back, this phrase came to me: *You're either in an identity crisis or your identity is in Christ.*

Whoa. I felt convicted.

Are you having an identity crisis? Or is your identity in Christ?

Putting our identity in Christ is the only way we're going to be able to choose NOW over NEXT. The same way we got here is the same way we're going to get through this: Jesus.

You're either in an identity crisis or your identity is in Christ.

When We Start Wishing We Could Go Back

This sentiment is mirrored in the story of Moses. Would you believe, when Moses finally managed to set the Israelites free (after 430 years of slavery), they started wishing they could go back to captivity?

Exodus 13 says, "When Pharaoh let the people go, God did not lead them on the road through the Philistine country, though that was shorter. For God said, 'If they face war, they might change their minds and return to Egypt.' So God led the people around by the desert road toward the Red Sea. The Israelites went up out of Egypt ready for battle" (vv. 17–18 NIV).

Shortly after this, God told Moses to tell the Israelites to turn back toward the sea. God said that He would harden Pharaoh's heart and that Pharaoh would go after the Israelites. God said that this would bring Him glory and the Egyptians would know that "I am the LORD" (14:1–4).

When the Israelites saw the Egyptians coming after them, they said to Moses: "Didn't we say to you in Egypt, 'Leave us alone; let us serve the Egyptians'? It would have been better for us to serve the Egyptians than to die in the desert!" (v. 12 NIV).

Moses responded, "Do not be afraid. Stand firm and you will see the deliverance the LORD will bring you today. The Egyptians you see today you will never see again. The LORD will fight for you; you need only to be still" (vv. 13–14 NIV).

After this, the angel of God stood behind them, and a pillar of cloud separated the people into two groups. Then, God used Moses to part the Red Sea, and the Israelites crossed through the sea safely. The Egyptians chased after them, but the Lord had Moses stretch

out his hands, causing the sea to return to normal as the waters rushed over the Egyptians, killing them all.

When we find ourselves wishing we could go back to our old lives, the ones that kept us enslaved in worldly ambitions, we have to make a conscious decision to let go of the way of the world and cling to His promises instead. This is hard work. This is like saying, "I don't care what this world offers me. I know He has what is best for me." This is something we have to choose daily.

We have to choose to remain in Him even when the rest of the world tells us we are missing out and falling behind. His light will lead us, and He will fill our hearts in ways the world never could. We can choose to whine (as I did that day in the shower), or we can remember WHO WON the battle between the Egyptians and the Israelites.

> *We have to choose to remain in Him even when the rest of the world tells us we are missing out and falling behind.*

When the Israelites chose to cling to God and remain faithful in Him, God did indeed fight for them. Can you imagine standing at the Red Sea as enemy forces bear down on you? Can you imagine God using Moses to make a pathway for you through the sea? Can you picture Him closing the pathway to destroy those who want to kill you?

God wants to use every step you take to bring honor and glory to His name.

Remember Paul, the guy who encountered Jesus and experienced radical transformation? He emphasized this same message in Romans 12:1–2:

> Therefore, I urge you, brothers and sisters, in view of God's mercy, to offer your bodies as a living sacrifice, holy and pleasing to God—this is your true and proper worship. Do not conform to the pattern of this world, but be transformed by the renewing of your mind. Then you will be able to test and approve what God's will is—his good, pleasing, and perfect will. (NIV)

Also, there's another guy in the Bible named Job. He faced extremely hard times and tremendous suffering. But even in pain, Job reminded us: "This is the way God works. Over and over again he pulls our souls back from certain destruction so we'll see the light—and *live* in the light!" (Job 33:29–30 MSG).

Made to Show His Light to the World

Speaking of light … Did you know that a butterfly's wings are made up of tiny, transparent scales? The color we are seeing is really just light. Did you catch that? The most beautiful part of the butterfly actually has nothing to do with the butterfly and everything to do with the *light*.

The same is true about our identity.

What is light? John 8:12 says, "Again Jesus spoke to them, saying, 'I am the light of the world. Whoever follows me will not walk in darkness, but will have the light of life.'"

Who we are and who we show to the world has nothing to do with us and everything to do with JESUS. We were made to shine *His light* so that the entire world could give Jesus *glory* (Matthew 5:16). Our lives are meant to *reflect Him* and *put Him on display*.

I want to take some pressure off of us here. We actually don't have to figure out who we are. All we have to do is show up where we are NOW, as God created us, and show the whole world who Jesus is. We don't have to put on a front or try to be like anyone else. We are small and insignificant without God's love. We are nothing without His light, and that is the very thing we need the world to see through our lives.

This is what is so beautiful about living in this new way. No amount of worldly success or accomplishments would ever qualify us for the *love* God gives us. We are nothing without *His light* shining in and through us.

Jesus is *light,* and Jesus plus nothing is *everything now.*

When most species of butterflies take flight, they only have a few weeks to live. Butterflies would be extinct if they wasted time clinging to the past, crawling around and wishing they were more like the caterpillars they used to be.

What are you going to do with this new you? Are you going to revert back to who you once were? Are you going to blame God for taking away the old you and feel sorry for yourself in the struggle?

Or ... are you going to use your life to reflect *His light* to the world around you?

We don't have time to waste either. NOW is the time.

James 4:13–15 says: "Now I have a word for you who brashly announce, 'Today—at the latest, tomorrow—we're off to such and such a city for the year. We're going to start a business and make a lot of money.' You don't know the first thing about tomorrow. You're nothing but a wisp of fog, catching a brief bit of sun before disappearing. Instead, make it a habit to say, 'If the Master wills it and we're still alive, we'll do this or that'" (MSG).

I don't care if you are reading this in a prison cell or a sorority house or a corporate office or a classroom, Jesus is right there with you NOW. He's waiting to reflect *His light* to the people around you.

Did you know ... that at the last minute, I rewrote this entire book? I didn't want to be vulnerable my first time writing it. I didn't want to tell you about the ugly part of me.

But vulnerability creates relational equity. It unlocks freedom and gives us eyes to see the NEW thing Jesus stands ready for us to do NOW.

Once I was able to set down my armor and open my heart in this vulnerable way, being authentic and honest about my personal struggles, then I was able to spread my wings and let His light transform me into this new Hope.

It is time to put *His light* on display. It is time to show the world your broken pieces that He has crafted together so beautifully. It is time to put NOW over NEXT once and for all.

NOW Over NEXT

I am not going to be able to leave you with every single answer. You won't close this book with a list of steps to conquer FOMO. But I will tell you that God doesn't call us to something He isn't going to equip us to do.

Caterpillars don't have great eyesight. God created them to only see what is right in front of them. If they needed to see far away to fly, don't you think He would have given them the ability to do so? If you needed to know everything about your life, don't you think He would have handed you a road map when you were born?

The Bible tells us that God's Word is a lamp to our feet and a light to our path (Psalm 119:105). There is something sweet about a lamp. We turn to our lamps when we need a safe place—a place we trust.

Jesus is the one we are going to have to walk with and trust as we embrace our new NOW.

The key to conquering FOMO once and for all is trusting Him. He knows everything about you. He knows your work ethic. He knows your desires. He knows what excites you. He knows what scares you out of your mind. He knows what comforts you. He knows your plans. He knows what is up against you. He knows what worries you have. He knows what you love.

When we do life with Jesus, we don't have to know every single next step. We don't have to be able to see far into the future. We just need His Word to guide us moment by moment.

We were made to see NOW.

We were made to be present NOW.

We were made to shine *His* light to the world NOW.

Are you ready for our last fun fact about butterflies? They don't flap their wings like a bird. They CLAP! They celebrate. This reminds me of what Paul says: "Celebrate God all day, every day. I mean, *revel* in him! Make it as clear as you can to all you meet that you're on their side, working with them and not against them. Help them see that the Master is about to arrive. He could show up any minute!" (Philippians 4:4–5 MSG).

The only way to step into the NOW without having an identity crisis is to put on the identity of Christ. The identity of Christ is *light*. All we have to do is wake up to where He has us and reflect His *light*.

That's it! That's all we are called to do.

> *NOW may seem small and insignificant compared to what we want NEXT to look like, but as you live out a life centered on Jesus and put His light on display for the whole world to see, there is nothing small and insignificant about what He has called you to do.*

Paul goes on to say, "Don't fret or worry. Instead of worrying, pray. Let petitions and praises shape your worries into prayers, letting God know your concerns. Before you know it, a sense of God's wholeness, everything coming together for good, will come and settle you down. It's wonderful what happens when Christ displaces worry at the center of your life" (vv. 6–7 MSG).

You have no idea what God has in store for you. Here's a sneak peek of what it's going to look like:

- **To Gain, You Must Lose**
  "Whoever would save his life will lose it, but whoever loses his life for my sake will save it."
  (Luke 9:24)

- **True Leadership Is in Serving Others**
  "It shall not be so among you. But whoever would be great among you must be your servant."
  (Mark 10:43)

- **To Be First, Be the Last**
  "He sat down and called the twelve. And he said to them, 'If anyone would be first, he must be last of all and servant of all.'" (Mark 9:35)

- **The Poor Are Rich in Faith**
  "Listen, my beloved brothers, has not God chosen those who are poor in the world to be rich in faith and heirs of the kingdom, which he has promised to those who love him?" (James 2:5)

- **In Weakness, You Find Strength**
  "For the sake of Christ, then, I am content with weaknesses, insults, hardships, persecutions, and

calamities. For when I am weak, then I am strong."
(2 Corinthians 12:10)

- **The Exalted Will Be Humbled**
  "Whoever exalts himself will be humbled, and whoever humbles himself will be exalted."
  (Matthew 23:12)

- **To Live, You Must Die to Self**
  "I have been crucified with Christ. It is no longer I who live, but Christ who lives in me. And the life I now live in the flesh I live by faith in the Son of God, who loved me and gave himself for me."
  (Galatians 2:20)

- **Anyone Who Loses Their Life Will Preserve It**
  "Whoever seeks to preserve his life will lose it, but whoever loses his life will keep it." (Luke 17:33)

- **The Greatest Is the Servant**
  "The greatest among you shall be your servant."
  (Matthew 23:11)

- **Hungering Leads to Satisfaction**
  "Blessed are those who hunger and thirst for righteousness, for they shall be satisfied."
  (Matthew 5:6)

- **Blessing Comes from Persecution**
  "Blessed are those who are persecuted for righteousness' sake, for theirs is the kingdom of heaven." (Matthew 5:10)

- **Rejoice in Suffering**
  "Not only that, but we rejoice in our sufferings, knowing that suffering produces endurance, and endurance produces character, and character produces hope." (Romans 5:3–4)

Have you ever heard of the "butterfly effect"? This theory was coined by a meteorologist named Edward Lorenz who explained that a butterfly flapping its wings in Brazil could cause a tornado in Texas. He was trying to prove that tiny, seemingly insignificant actions can set off a chain of events that result in *big changes* and have *big impacts*.

NOW may seem small and insignificant compared to what we want NEXT to look like, but as you live out a life centered on Jesus and put *His light* on display for the whole world to see, there is nothing small and insignificant about what He has called you to do.

I believe every single small step you take with Jesus is going to illuminate the plans, purpose, and freedom that you never knew existed. I believe you're going to see your brokenness as something beautiful. I believe God is going to redeem the missteps and mistakes you've made to break other people free from things they're stuck in. I believe you're going to conquer the fear of missing out once and for all.

Embrace the Now

1. How can you let go of who you once were and step into what God is doing now?

2. Write out what your normal day-to-day looks like. Now, write out how you can shine your LIGHT and reflect Jesus in each of those spaces.

3. How would you describe what God has been doing in your life through this message of *Now Over Next*?

4. What have you learned?

5. How has your perspective changed?

6. What aha moments have you had?

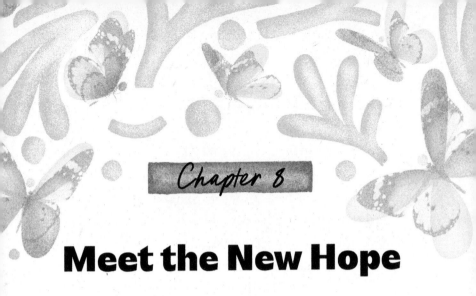

Chapter 8

Meet the New Hope

There is something in the picture of the old Hope in front of the Taj Mahal that sticks out to me like a sore thumb. If I were a betting girl, I'd say there was no way you caught on to it. It looks legit and made me look like I had really "made it." But what would you think if I told you that the luxurious Louis Vuitton purse I was proudly carrying was … a fake? Yep, it wasn't real. It was a knockoff.

As I reflect back on the old Hope, I can see so many ironies between that fake Louis and my old life. Like the purse, the *atta-girl*s, titles, and praise that I carried around with me were … meaningless. The purse was flashy and was made to be seen. I lived the same way.

Now that the old Hope is gone, I can see that the way I was living, like the value of the purse, was meaningless. Those objects and opinions had no real value. The thrill of each new acquisition or accomplishment quickly faded away and left me just about as filled up as the hollows of that big, fancy purse.

I have a hard time coming up with the words to tell you about the new Hope, so I'll share a story.

Will recently woke up in the middle of the night and said, "Hope, go get the girls. I'll get Remi. We have to go."

I quickly woke and asked, "What's going on?"

"A tornado. It's heading right toward us. We have about ten minutes to get out of its way," Will explained.

I immediately ran upstairs to wake our three out-of-town visitors, Jaden, Trinity, and Hilary, who had been helping launch my Purpose Doesn't Pause nonprofit. They jumped to their feet, and we all rushed to Will's truck. Talk about team bonding!

The old Hope might have rushed through the house grabbing my laptop, cell phone, and … maybe even that fancy handbag. But the new Hope didn't grab a single thing. I didn't even take my cell phone. I felt at peace with leaving every material thing behind.

> *We are here. Now. Not caring one bit about what might happen. Next.*

As we drove south, away from the tornado, I looked around the truck at my husband, daughter, friends, and our goldendoodle, Sadie. Even if we lost *everything* we'd left behind, I felt tremendous peace knowing I still had *everything* that mattered. And most importantly, I had Jesus.

That's the new Hope!

Here's a picture of me reading a book with my daughter, Remi, so you can see the difference for yourself. I'm sporting my natural brown hair, wearing worn-out overalls with a yogurt-stained shirt from Remi's little fingers, and sitting on the floor of our living room. I'm focused on enjoying my time with Remi, and our faces show that we're both completely in the moment. We aren't worried about what the rest of the world is up to or what we're missing out on. We are here. Now. Not caring one bit about what might happen. Next.

Kyra Noel Photography

Like leaving my cell phone and belongings the night of the storm, I've left behind the way I used to live. In the same way I rushed to the truck to avoid a tornado, I'm urgently doing whatever I feel led to do NOW.

I no longer fix my eyes on the future.
Instead, I fix my eyes on the One who will take care of me for eternity.

I no longer feel this pressure to try to be something bigger than I am.
Instead, I want my life to reflect the One who is the God of the universe.

I no longer need to be seen by this world.
Instead, I am grateful to know that God sees me. Any role He gives me is greater than I deserve.

There is no such thing as missing out when we are doing life with Jesus. Every moment is a gift, and the Giver is good! Just as the old Hope has gone, and the new Hope is here, I believe the NEW is here waiting on you NOW.

Second Corinthians 5:16–20 says it best:

> Because of this decision we don't evaluate people
> by what they have or how they look. We looked at
> the Messiah that way once and got it all wrong, as

you know. We certainly don't look at him that way anymore. Now we look inside, and what we see is that anyone united with the Messiah gets a fresh start, is created new. **The old life is gone; a new life emerges!** Look at it! All this comes from the God who settled the relationship between us and him, and then called us to settle our relationships with each other. God put the world square with himself through the Messiah, giving the world a fresh start by offering forgiveness of sins. God has given us the task of telling everyone what he is doing. We're Christ's representatives. God uses us to persuade men and women to drop their differences and enter into God's work of making things right between them. We're speaking for Christ himself now: Become friends with God; he's already a friend with you. (MSG)

If you're looking for me, you can find me in your corner cheering you on! Here's to choosing NOW over NEXT.

Embrace the Now

1. How would you describe the old you?

2. How would you describe the new you?

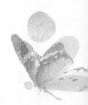

3. Are there any stories or examples that have allowed you to see a difference between the old and the new you?

4. What are you excited about NOW?

5. How have you conquered the fear of missing out?

6. Use this space to write a prayer to God as you step into NOW over NEXT.

A Prayer As You Step into NOW

I can't thank you enough for going on this journey with me. Before you step into what God is doing now, can we say a prayer together?

Dear God,

Thank You for our time together—with You, in these pages. Lord, as we step into what You are doing now, please give us strength and boldness. Continue to transform us.

On the days that are hard, meet us and lift us up, please. On the days that are good, give us courage to share Your name and give all the glory to You.

We want our lives to look different. You have changed us, and we want our lives to display Your goodness and restoration for all to see.

Help us to step into what You are doing now in a way we never have. Give us the opportunity to share what You are doing. Surprise us with ways to make Your name known in the everyday, ordinary places.

Our lives are *yours*. Right NOW is *yours*.

Let Your will be done. Let Your kingdom come. We are ready for this moment. Give us eyes to see and ears to hear. We are an army of women rising up to make heaven crowded.

We love you and praise you.

In Jesus' name, amen!

Stories That Spark HOPE

Welcome to the section of stories that spark HOPE! There is nothing more encouraging to me than seeing God's restoration and faithfulness shine through the lives of other people. So I've included testimonies from women who inspire me and point me to Jesus. I hope these stories spark HOPE and encourage you to keep going!

From Advancing Her Career to Advancing His Kingdom
with Jackie Johnson

I'm so excited for you to meet my friend Jackie Johnson. She's strong and mighty with a confidence that comes from the Lord. I hope her story can encourage you to step into the abundant life God has for you today.

Hope: Jackie, when did you first realize there could be more to life than the way you were living?

Jackie: I had moved from Oklahoma to California for a career in retail management. I had been advancing with CVS and Walgreens, and I thought I was doing everything right. I lived near Newport Beach, a mile from the Pacific Coast Highway. I wore high heels and had all the superficial things any woman my age could possibly have wanted. I felt like I had stepped into everything we're told to work for in life.

Over the span of three months, I was helping and managing more than seventeen stores. I was climbing the corporate ladder and had reached a high-level managerial position. Not only was I sent to help other stores through troubled times, but I was also helping tackle loss prevention and breaking down the criminal rings that sold pharmaceuticals or stole prescriptions from our stores. I was trying to be everything for everyone. And I was exhausted.

Then, I started feeling sick, and I realized there might be more to life than this "best life" I'd been living.

Hope: What perspective shifts did you have?

Jackie: I didn't know why I was getting sick because, remember, I had it all. I thought that all my success was because of my own ability. I was prideful.

Also, FOMO had its grip on me. I feared that if I didn't continue working so hard, I wouldn't have enough money. I wouldn't be able to afford to live in such a beautiful place. I feared if I stopped, then I would lose all the material possessions I had built up and stored away.

I kept working. And my health declined more and more. I continued ignoring it, fueling my way through fifteen-hour workdays by taking caffeine pills. One day, I woke up and my skin was burning. For more than a year, I had been battling a rash by putting a prescriptive cream over it and carrying on with my life. But now, when I looked in the mirror, the rash covered me head to toe.

Then my hair started falling out. Still, I kept going ... until I got injured at work.

Hope: That's intense. So, what did you do next?

Jackie: The injury was severe, so I had to stop working for a year and a half. It took this to make me slow down long enough to realize there was more to life than the way I'd been living. If the way I was living was going to take my life away, I didn't want it. I no longer cared about the money. It was no longer fulfilling because I was too sick to enjoy it.

Hope: I relate to your story so much because it was during maternity leave when I realized there was more to life than climbing the corporate ladder. Tell me a little about this year and a half when you couldn't work.

Jackie: I didn't recognize myself in the mirror. I was broken physically, mentally, socially, and financially. But I was especially broken spiritually. I'm a pastor's kid who had grown up in church. I knew God's Word, but I had stepped away from it because I'd become so caught up with the world.

During this time, I returned to God. I said, "God, I need You to remake me."

Doctors couldn't help me. They didn't have answers. God was the only one I could turn to.

I said, "God, You created every cell in my body … every fiber of mine. I need You to make me whole."

I started reading the Word of God, singing, and praising Him in the pain. Although it wasn't a quick fix, God started healing and repairing me.

Hope: What did you end up doing after all of this?

Jackie: I started sharing my health journey and talking to others about what God was doing in me. Instead of returning to my other job, I started my own business helping people get healthy. I converted my condo into a gym and trained people at the park. It was a merger

of the business-side skill set I had developed through the years and my newfound passion for wellness.

Hope: I love how you took the gifts He gave you and used them for His good and glory. Can you share your thoughts on this?

Jackie: We can either use the gifts He has given us to advance ourselves, or we can steward them to help others. Jesus used His gifts to serve others. He washed people's feet. He sat with the poor.

Like Jesus, we have a choice. We can live for ourselves, or we can use our gifts to serve others.

Hope: When I say the present is the present, what does that make you think of? How do you live this out in your daily life?

Jackie: He only promises us our daily bread. He tells us not to worry about tomorrow. Now, I live every day with the goal of serving others. My values are faith, family, and service. I try to walk through each day living out those values.

But the Bible shows us that no one who truly served God had an easy life. Esther was tested. Ruth was tested. Noah was tested. Moses was tested. Jesus was tested. The list goes on. Hardship comes with serving Christ. So when life starts to feel too easy for me, I stop and look to see who I'm serving. Am I serving myself or God?

From Loss to Light
with Ashtynne Kirk

One of the first things "new Hope" did was turn to a dietician named Ashtynne for help in getting my physical health restored. When Ashtynne and I connected, I sensed that we had been brought together for something bigger than getting my health back on track. The more we talked, the more she shared her story with me.

I immediately felt admiration not only for her intellect and skill set but also because she was intentional and encouraging. I hope her story meets you wherever you are and points you to the goodness of God.

Hope: Tell us about your faith journey and how your life started to look and feel different.

Ashtynne: I would describe my walk with Christ as a sweet and gentle unraveling. I grew up in church; however, while I was in college, I felt a pull to draw nearer to God.

Unfortunately, that changed when I found myself facing a difficult, high-risk pregnancy that led to me delivering my second son, Graham, stillborn.

That experience felt as though I ran into Jesus like a brick wall—fully surrendering my circumstances, finding unnatural joy and peace in Him regardless of the outcome, trusting Him completely, and feeling His all-consuming love and comfort through it all.

Holding my son's still body, knowing that he was dancing with Jesus, gave me a deeper understanding of His love for me.

My favorite passage at this time in my life was Psalm 62:5–8, which says, "Yes, my soul, find rest in God; my hope comes from him. Truly he is my rock and my salvation; he is my fortress, I will not be shaken. My salvation and my honor depend on God; he is my mighty rock, my refuge. Trust in him at all times, you people; pour out your hearts to him, for God is our refuge" (NIV).

Hope: **I can't imagine what you went through. I'm so sorry, Ashtynne. Was there a particular moment that God showed you He was doing something new in you?**

Ashtynne: My faith became real to me when I had Graham. I'll never forget the first Communion I took part in after losing Graham. It was the sweetest encounter with the Lord. I realized in that moment the incredible amount of love God has for me. He walked through the grief with me. I felt immense love from God in that moment. I could see His love for us in a whole new way. I couldn't imagine the love and sacrifice He'd made to send His Child to die for us.

Hope: **How has your perspective changed? How does life look different for you now?**

Ashtynne: During my grief, I told Mom I was never going to read anything Paul wrote in the Bible because he basically tells us to be

happy even when things are hard. I remember saying, "That's stupid. I'm not happy. I'm not reading what he has to say." My mom said, "It's okay; you'll grow through that." She was right.

I started really reading the Word and began to understand what Paul was trying to tell us. After losing Graham, I experienced how Jesus can give us joy in seasons of hardship. I began to see how beautiful Jesus is, even while I was in turmoil. I read my Bible consistently during this time because I was desperate and had nothing else but Jesus, which I'm very thankful for because I don't want anything else other than Jesus right now.

Hope: That's so good. Tell us how you were able to find joy and allow God to do a new thing through such an unimaginable situation. What helped you that you'd like to share with others?

Ashtynne: I would talk to Jesus anytime I was alone—sometimes that was after my first son, Joseph, was asleep. Other times I was in the shower or driving in my car. I couldn't really process what God was doing or saying unless I was by myself and ready to listen.

But finding that time to be alone with God was a challenge because, even in the deepest grief, I was still a mother and I was working. My life never stopped after I lost Graham. I didn't have a postpartum period. I didn't have "maternity leave." I had to continue living my life as if nothing had happened, as if I hadn't just given birth to a stillborn baby.

I remember praying and saying, "I don't have any idea what to do. I don't have any idea how I'm feeling right now. This is all just too

much for me." I would tell Him and sit ready to listen and allow Him to work on my heart through the Holy Spirit.

A huge reason I had peace and was able to go to God with this is because of a prayer my mom prayed over me. I called my mom when I was going into labor. She was driving to Texas to be with me, and we didn't know what was going to happen. The outcome wasn't looking very good, but we didn't yet know that Graham was going to lose his life.

My mom was praying that the enemy wouldn't win or get any glory from this situation. That prayer is what still motivates me to lean on God and have peace. I felt like the enemy would have gotten glory and won if I felt so broken that I couldn't see the goodness of God. The enemy wants us to doubt and to question God and to be mad at God in our situations. I decided I wasn't going to allow the enemy to use this situation. God is good and the enemy is not.

I'm pregnant again now. From this experience, I can say that God is good regardless of the situation we are walking through.

From Feeling Hopeless to Believing for Abundantly More
with Sarah Hallas Lima

Right before *Purpose Doesn't Pause* came out, Sarah Hallas Lima reached out to me and said that the Lord had put it on her heart to come alongside me to help me share my story on social media. What Sarah didn't know was that I had been praying and asking God to bring someone to help me. Her offer was an answered prayer.

Sarah's humility and faith has strengthened my own faith in ways words could never express. On the days when I question what God is up to, Sarah gently reminds me of how faithful God is to provide and how He has already gone before me. I can't wait for you to read her story!

Hope: **Tell us about a time your world came crashing down.**

Sarah: When the world shut down during the pandemic, I found myself in the middle of a divorce. I kept asking God, "What do You have next for me?"

Experiencing this type of rejection was my worst nightmare. I felt like a failure and had no clue where I had gone so wrong. My life looked like something I never ever would have imagined.

A friend I had met online (and had never met in person) gave me a call one day. She said, "Hey, the world is shutting down, and I lost my job. I need to do something different, and I'm thinking about moving to Nashville."

Broken and alone, I said, "Do you need a roommate? I'm in the middle of a divorce, and I don't know what to do next."

Just like that … I moved from Florida to Nashville. When people would ask what had brought me to Nashville, I didn't want to go into the whole story about my divorce, so I'd reply: "I feel like God's going to do something really big."

I don't know what exactly it was, but everything lined up perfectly for me to get to Nashville. I couldn't have found a cheaper flight, our first month's rent at our apartment was free, and I got a random restaurant job. It was so clear that I was supposed to be there.

Less than six weeks later, I found out I was six months pregnant with my son, Harv. People asked me, "How did you not know you were pregnant?" Trust me. I really didn't know.

One day I was looking at a picture of myself, and I thought I was gaining a little bit of weight, but I felt fine. I'd been so stressed, so overwhelmed, so devastated by the divorce that I hadn't really noticed the changes in my own body. All of a sudden, it clicked in my brain that maybe I should take a pregnancy test. It showed "positive" immediately.

I told some of my friends, and they were freaking out. They immediately asked what I was going to do. They wanted to know if I was okay and if I needed to go back to Florida.

Despite their panic, I remember having so much peace.

Hope: Talk us through how you were able to find hope and peace while going through a divorce and learning you were six months pregnant.

Sarah: When I saw those two pink lines, I was instantly aware that there was absolutely no way I could get through this situation without God. This was my worst nightmare. The world was still battling the COVID pandemic. The government was mailing stimulus checks here and there, but I was mainly depending on my bartending job. Now that I realized I was pregnant, my plans completely changed.

When people ask me this question, I don't even know how to articulate it. I believe without a shadow of a doubt that God is kind and allows us to be in situations bigger than us so we can do life with Him. I had no choice here but to believe He had a bigger and better plan than what I could see in that moment.

He really started to speak to me through the verse Ephesians 3:20, which says, "Now to him who is able to do far more abundantly than all that we ask or think, according to the power at work within us." The phrase "abundantly more" has been such a staple in my life because I had to tell myself through this that God is going to do bigger and better than what I could ask, think, or imagine.

I never thought I would have ended up divorced, pregnant, and bartending in Nashville. Up until that point, I had been born and raised in a Christian home. I had attended church and done all the "right" things, but my faith had not become real to me until it was just me and God facing this situation. Until then, my life had been good, even during hard times. But this! This totally changed my life.

God gave me peace and hope in my darkest moments. He was there with me.

Hope: Is there a particular Bible story that showed you God's character and gave you the hope you needed to walk through this?

Sarah: I was encouraged by the story of Joseph and how God took him from prison to a position of power.

Joseph had a pretty "unfair" life. He was betrayed and sold into slavery by his brothers. He was wrongfully accused and thrown into prison. He was forgotten by the one person who had the ability to set him free. I'm sure he was asking God, "What did I do to deserve this?"

Yet, along the way, Joseph continued to faithfully serve his fellow prisoners with his gift of dream interpretation. Until, years later, Joseph was summoned to interpret Pharaoh's dream. This resulted in Pharaoh putting Joseph into a position of power over Egypt.

Joseph had experienced one painful disappointment after another and had been knocked down in life. But then, overnight, he'd gone from being wrongfully imprisoned to being recognized for his God-given gifts and set in a place of power by the pharaoh. I resonated with his story so much.

Despite all his sufferings, Joseph stayed faithful to God and honored the gifts God had given him. Then, when Pharaoh needed him, he was ready.

All those difficult seasons he'd endured had never been intended as punishment after all. God had been using them as preparation, strengthening Joseph and making him wiser and more resilient so that when the time came, he would be ready to lead.

The same is true for you.

Overnight, Joseph's circumstances changed because he was prepared. He couldn't have done that unless he had stayed faithful through the difficult seasons. Even when there was no hope. When Pharaoh asked Joseph how he was so wise, Joseph gave all the glory to God. This inspired me to stay close to the Lord, knowing I had no clue what He was preparing me for but that something better was ahead for me.

Even at your lowest, the Lord is preparing you for something better than you could ask, think, or imagine. Trust me, I know when things don't go according to plan, it's easy to focus on our disappointment, which is where the enemy sneaks in and plants seeds of fear, self-doubt, regret, bitterness, resentment, or whatever else you're wrestling with right now.

I'm begging you—do not let them take root. This very season has a supernatural purpose: to prepare you for something better.

I want to challenge you today to consider if, like Joseph, your situation was to change to the best-case scenario tomorrow, what would you do differently today? How would you carry yourself, what would you prioritize, and where would you spend your time?

I know it can be tempting to make a plan to get out of your current situation ... but I need you to believe with me that God's going to do something even better. He's going to elevate your faith and deliver you a purposeful future. Trust in Him.

Hope: This next part of your testimony blows my mind. Share it with us.

Sarah: When I was finally in a good place of healing, I started praying for a husband. I had been going on dates and asked God, "What is this going to look like? I believe You designed families, and You don't want me raising Harv on my own. Who do You have for me to complete this?"

I prayed and I stayed faithful. There were guys who I wanted it to be, and God would be very clear that they weren't my future husband. Even when God would lead me to shut certain doors, I was still so confident that my future husband was going to be someone amazing.

All of this to say, the Lord had really started softening my heart toward my ex-husband, David. God told me to be praying for him and his future wife. I didn't think much about this because David was obviously going to be in Harv's life so that meant David would remain in my life.

David ended up asking if we could reconcile the past and work toward true forgiveness. I was grateful that the Lord had allowed us to understand each other, apologize, and communicate better. This allowed us to come together as a team and co-parent Harv.

When David planned to move to Tennessee to be closer to Harv, I had no intentions of getting back together with him. I was happy.

But when I saw David, he looked different to me. His demeanor was different, and I felt the Lord tell me, "That's your husband."

I'm not going to lie and say it was a dream come true. At first, I was thinking, *You've got to be kidding me.* We had forgiven each other enough to co-parent, but getting back together would require trust, communication, and an even deeper level of healing.

So, I wrestled. I have a note in my phone that looks like two people having a conversation, but it's just me going back and forth between why I should and shouldn't get back together with David. But, ultimately, my heart wanted God's will, and it was clear that David and I were meant to be together.

David and I remarried, and the day before we celebrated our one-year wedding anniversary, we found out we were pregnant with baby number two. Now, I'm walking through my pregnancy with David and Harv as we're preparing for the arrival of our daughter. It is such a picture of God's unseen plans for all of us.

From Goals to Discovering God's Greater Plan

with Jaden McNair

My first encounter with Jaden McNair took me by surprise. After I hosted my first "Purpose Doesn't Pause Gathering," she came up to me and said, "The Lord just put it on my heart to come and tell you that I have extra time this semester. I want to help you."

I remember saying, "Are you serious? I need help!"

Wise beyond her years, Jaden encouraged me to run to what the Lord was inviting us into. I hope her story will inspire you too.

Hope: Tell us about a time you experienced FOMO.

Jaden: I was the girl in high school who was dead set on attending a certain college while everyone around me was completely clueless. During my junior and senior years, I truly got to watch the Lord go before me in all things and plant me at my dream school: Ouachita Baptist University (OBU).

He opened doors to meet financial needs, gave me peace on visits, and began sowing community before I ever got there. My best friend was my suitemate, and the Lord gave me the sweetest roommate. Move-in day was a dream, and all the blessings of the school were now mine. I was studying premed with an end goal of becoming a pediatrician specializing in neonatal care.

My studies were rigorous, but nothing could have prepared me for the essay I had to write for my freshman seminar class. The essay

was no huge task, but it led me directly to the feet of Jesus. The prompt was simple: Write about the giftings the Lord has given you and how those gifts will be stewarded in your future career.

Let's just say this paper revealed that premed was not what the Lord was calling me to.

I quickly hit rock bottom when I realized the Lord may have something else in store for me. All my plans went out the window when I wrote the last few lines of the paper: "I'm not sure what the Lord has for me, but I know it's not this."

So there I was, just a few months into college, confused and questioning.

I vividly remember sitting in my car in the dorm parking lot crying to my mom over FaceTime because it felt like everything I'd ever wanted was instantly gone. In this conversation we began talking about other options the Lord may have for me, and I ultimately decided to change my major to nursing.

Knowing I was being called to vocational ministry in some capacity, this major would allow me to pursue the medical passions the Lord has given me while also providing time to steward ministry opportunities.

It sounds like my life problems were all solved on that FaceTime call with my mom, but this wrestle was just the beginning.

Hope: **So you were living in the middle of your dream only to discover that God was clearly calling you elsewhere. What did you do next?**

Jaden: It took a hot minute for me to gain my composure enough to walk back into my dorm. I walked in, sat on my bed, and instantly began to stress about all the unknowns that lay ahead.

This corner became my safe space for the rest of that semester. It's where I got to meet the Lord with my questions and doubts. It's where I applied to the school in my hometown that I'd never thought I'd attend. It's where I prayed for opportunities to provide room for me to break the news to my best friends. It's where I got to intimately know my Father. Psalm 37 was a passage I referenced often in this little corner.

This season was one of surrender. Knowing I didn't have the answers, I trusted that God did and that I could rest. The Lord delights in the details of our lives, and that corner is a testament of that truth. While I spent many hours in this corner, my day-to-day life didn't change. I was still a college student, still overwhelmed with work, and still homesick.

I spent nearly every weekend driving home. My last month was sad and depressing because my dorm room felt like a hotel, but the Lord opened my eyes to see the blessing Ouachita had given me. Friends I would have never met, mentors and professors who I will forever cherish, and so many late nights full of memories in the science building.

Hope: It is always those random, unexpected moments that change everything. What happened when you surrendered everything to God?

Jaden: The moment of full surrender was my drive home on December 16. Some of my family had helped me pack up the rest of my things, my final exams were over, and I drove off campus no longer a Tiger. It was a bittersweet moment. Full of expectations for what the Lord had planned, but with so much sadness for the long-held dream I was walking away from.

Goodbyes are always hard, but saying bye to my dream was such a pruning moment. Christmas break was interesting, as I was no longer at OBU but also not yet at UCA (University of Central Arkansas). I honestly felt a little stranded in the middle.

Doubt crept in, and my bed at my house became my new corner to seek the Lord. The holidays passed quickly, and before I knew it, I was moving into a dorm with my childhood best friend and starting all over again. Yes, I was at a college in my hometown, but all my high school friends had already had a semester's worth of friendships in motion.

Again, the Lord was faithful to meet me in my wrestle. I will never forget my first encounter as a UCA student. When I took a detour to say hey to a friend, the guy in front of me opened the door, made eye contact with me, and then proceeded to slam the door in my face.

It sounds silly, but at OBU guys will come running from behind to hold a door for you. A closed door in my face led me to have a moment with the Lord where I simply said, "Whatever You have for me and however You want to reveal it, I'm all in."

It's been a little over a year from this transition and, man, has the Lord done abundantly more than I could ever have imagined. Did I

"waste" a whole semester of classes? Maybe. Did I have to completely restart at my new college? Yeah. Did my wrestle hurt? Yes. Did God show up? Absolutely.

My life looks nothing like I thought it would. I thought I would be a premed student at OBU, having fun in a social club, making the most of being single and thriving in Jesus, living with my best friends, and doing it all at my dream school as I chased a medical career.

Instead, I'm serving in youth ministry, studying nursing, living alone, enjoying coffee dates with my people all day, helping my best friend start a podcast and nonprofit, and … I'm engaged!

Each of these in and of themselves are testimonies of the Lord's goodness. There is no life better than a life surrendered fully to whatever the Lord asks of you. He knows the gifts He has given you, and He's faithful to show you how to steward them. You will never regret surrendering it all. The "costs" are nothing when you compare it to His blessings that abound.

Hope: What would you tell the girl who is wrestling with God and struggling with FOMO today?

Jaden: Girl, we have all been there! One thing we have to remember when it comes to breaking free from anything the enemy throws our way is the authority of God. He is Jehovah Nissi—the Lord is our banner (Exodus 17). He alone defeated death and the grave, proclaiming victory! His victory extends to His children. We get to proclaim His victory, a victory that defeated the enemy!

So why are we letting things like FOMO have a say in our lives when we know God has already won the battle? We are on this earth for a greater purpose, and the enemy has no ground to let FOMO keep us from our true identity.

Second Timothy 1:7 says, "God gave us a spirit not of fear but of power and love and self-control." This truth reminds me that fear is not of the Lord, so why do we choose to live in a FOMO mentality? The Lord has us.

The season we are walking in is exactly where the Lord has placed us for this exact day and this exact time. John 16:33 says, "In the world you will have tribulation. But take heart; I have overcome the world."

From Intrusive Thoughts to Speaking Truth Over Your Situation

with Trinity Romesberg

Trinity Romesberg is full of joy and sits on the edge of her seat, expectant for what God is going to do. She is the friend who sees you and reminds you that God sees you too. She lets the Holy Spirit lead her, and I can't wait for you to learn from her story!

Hope: Can you tell us about a time in your life when you had a freak-out moment?

Trinity: Yes! When I went to college, I realized that the way I was raised and the faith I was pursuing made me feel really different from my peers and really alone. I quickly realized that I was either going to have to choose to be myself, or I was going to have to try to fit in with everyone else.

I chose to try to fit in with everyone else. I would go to parties and come home and cry because I felt like I didn't have a place. I struggled to go to church alone, and life felt really out of my control. In high school, I'd had so many friends and had experienced all the silly things like winning prom queen and homecoming queen. I felt like I had peaked in high school and life was never going to get any better than that.

This freak-out moment led me to start struggling with suicidal ideation. I knew I wanted to live, so I didn't understand why I was

feeling this way. I didn't understand why I was dealing with panic attacks or depression. I'd never struggled with any of this while I was growing up.

Hope: **That sounds hard to walk through. How did you overcome all of it?**

Trinity: I started turning to people in my life who were good influences. I'd ask my mom and my grandma for prayer. When I told them I didn't know what to do, they told me I needed to get back to my faith. That is when I realized I didn't know Jesus personally.

That whole freak-out season of my life had led to anxiety, depression, fear, and intrusive thoughts. I would google how to get better, but I soon realized that Google wasn't going to fix me. Only Jesus was going to fix me.

In the past, I had been the friend who people would come to for advice, and now I was the one looking for help. The last place I thought to turn to was Scripture, because if the Bible didn't specifically say words like *depression* or *suicidal ideation* in bold print, I didn't think that was the answer. I felt like I needed help right away. The world we live in makes us think we need instant fixes and instant gratification. I realized I had to spend time reading the Word and letting it soak in. The truth found in Scripture had to get to the core and the root of my heart first.

Hope: **What did God reveal to you?**

Trinity: This took a lot of self-evaluation. I remember saying, "Okay, God. I don't know how to get better, but if it is Your will, can You show me the root of where all of this started?"

God revealed to me that a lot of it was perfectionism. I held a lot of "people-pleasing" in my heart, and God showed me that this desire came from me wanting people to think I was a good person.

I remember in high school people would make remarks like "Oh, you're too fake" or "You're too much for people." I was constantly so worried that everyone was waiting for me to slip up or mess up. My really bad anxiety and intrusive thoughts told me that everyone was waiting for me to fall.

I asked God, "Can You give me relief from this?"

Through asking God for relief, He taught me that we have to figure out what matters to us. Is it going to be fear of man or is it going to be fear of God?

I think when people hear "fear of God," they think He's going to strike them down or something. To me, the fear of God is saying, "God, I'm in awe of who You are and I'm going to honor You with my life."

This allowed me to see that I don't need to prove myself to people. I don't need to be who they want me to be. I need to be who God has called me to be because that's the only opinion that matters at the end of the day. I'm serving and living for God.

Hope: What advice do you have for the one who is in the middle of a freak-out moment?

Trinity: I think it's asking yourself: Who are you serving?

There are still times when fear, anxiety, and intrusive thoughts creep into my mind. But now I know how to fight it. Here would be my advice for the one who finds herself facing those battles today:

- Speak with authority and truth over the things that are causing you to freak out. The Bible tells us to take our thoughts captive to make them obedient to Christ (2 Corinthians 10:5).
- Spend time in the Word. Find a Bible story you can relate to.

Jesus tells us, "I have given you authority to trample on snakes and scorpions and to overcome all the power of the enemy; nothing will harm you" (Luke 10:19 NIV).

Know that your power comes from God, not from your own strength. Through the power and authority God has given you, you can step on any negative thoughts and fears that are coming from the enemy.

Hope: What advice do you have for the one who doesn't understand why this is happening to them?

Trinity: I think you have to really evaluate your heart. Something I really struggled with in this season is why all of this was happening to me. I was so scared to tell people I was going through a hard time

because I thought that made me weak. It really does take a lot of humility and heart work to get through the freak-out moments.

Sometimes it feels like there is stigma attached to not being okay. We start to think, *What's wrong with me?*

I want to encourage you that there is nothing wrong with you. There's an enemy who is out to kill, steal, and destroy your peace, your joy, and your hope (John 10:10).

If it wasn't for my freak-out moment, I wouldn't have become the vulnerable, open person I am today.

Keep your eyes on Jesus. Keep your eyes locked on the truth found in His Word. Don't give up on praying for healing over your situation. Paul talks about God's power being made perfect in our weakness (2 Corinthians 12:9). When you are weak, He is strong.

Believe and have faith that God can do anything. Don't be stuck thinking you don't deserve healing. Just keep talking to Jesus.

From Valleys to God's Victory
with Hilary Davies

Hilary Davies joined a mentorship group I was leading, and every time she would speak, God was so clearly in her heart. Today, she is running the strategy and operations for Purpose Doesn't Pause (on top of working her full-time job and being a wife and a mom to two of the cutest little girls). Hilary is a servant leader and will do anything to spread the Word of God. God has given her a gift of stewarding His momentum and pushing His plans forward in a beautiful way.

Hope: **Tell us about a season in your life when you felt like you couldn't catch a break.**

Hilary: I recently faced three different hardships back-to-back, three years in a row. Each situation tested my faith. Like a series of crossroads, each time I had a choice to make. I could place my trust in the world, or I could follow a path that placed full trust in God. Each time, I went where God was calling me, even though I was walking into the unknown.

In 2020, my marriage faced a hardship of broken trust and a misuse of finances. My sense of security was ripped out from under me, and it sent me into an immediate spiral. Devastated, I anchored into God's Word and turned to Him for peace. Eventually, I experienced beautiful healing in my marriage. Knowing I had made it out of the worst, I focused forward.

Well, in 2021, I faced the next crisis when my job became threatened. I had put my heart and soul into this company, and this felt again as if the security was being ripped out from under me. After deep prayer, I chose the path that God was calling me to, and again He delivered complete resolve in that situation. I was able to keep my job.

The following year, my family endured yet another financial scare. This time we were faced with an oil spill on our property. Overnight, we were facing hundreds of thousands of dollars in damage, our home's foundation was at risk, and a stream beside our house was being polluted.

Hope: Your testimonies are truly inspiring. Tell us how you walked through them and what God did for you and your family.

Hilary: This oil spill was a scary situation for our family, putting our financial security at risk—again. I prayed *boldly* that God would use this situation however He needed to, fully for His good.

I couldn't think too far ahead, which was the exact opposite of my usual reaction. My innate reaction would be to plan and strategize solutions. My innermost desire has always been to find security.

This time, however, there was no immediate solution to be found. I had to pause and surrender everything to God. Leaning into a heart of worship allowed me to step into His plan for me.

Hope: **Walk us through the most recent hardship in more detail.**

Hilary: When we faced the oil spill, we faced hundreds of thousands of dollars for remediation. We were advised to seek legal counsel and to submit our claim to insurance. The odds of the insurance company approving the claim were next to none, and they denied us twice.

Yet, I refused to give up. I prayed and I worshipped. I trusted God had a plan. I knew where I had to place my energy and faith in those moments.

Despite our financial strains, we remained obedient in our tithing. I would think about Matthew 6:33–34, which says, "Seek first the kingdom of God and his righteousness, and all these things will be added to you. Therefore do not be anxious about tomorrow, for tomorrow will be anxious for itself. Sufficient for the day is its own trouble."

It was in these moments of prayer and worship that I decided to praise Him and thank Him for all He had *already* delivered in my life. The verse I stood on during this time was Philippians 4:6: "Do not be anxious about anything, but in everything by prayer and supplication with thanksgiving let your requests be made known to God."

I made my bold request known, that He USE the situation however He intended it, for His glory. I told Him I trusted in His greater purpose.

I cried out in full trust of His promise and His abundance, knowing that whatever my portion would be in the end, it would be enough. I was prepared to lose everything. Yes, even my home. I had come from nothing, so I could easily go right back.

And so, I worshipped.

Well, let me tell you ... God came through far beyond my imagination. Would you believe our insurance company called us back after I submitted a *third* claim. After denying us twice already, somehow, someway, they were now going to cover the costs to the point where no one, not even our legal counsel, could explain it!

Only God.

Hope: How were you able to see past the fear and worship as if God had already provided?

Hilary: At first, I asked, "God, why? Why are we going through this? We have already endured other situations these past couple of years, Lord. Why this now? Another test of faith? Really?"

But then I asked myself, "Who do I think I am?"

I quickly pivoted, talking to Him through my tears and saying, "Okay, God. Whatever this is that I'm going through, use it for Your glory. I have no idea what the plan is here, but I trust in You. Even if we lose all our money and possessions, please help me bring You glory through this."

I knew right then, after the wrestle, that I was "on the line" to be used by God. I had a peace about it. Little did I know I would be

sharing my testimony like this. God is a God of a greater plan, and He makes the impossible possible.

Hope: **What encouragement do you have for the one who feels like she can't catch a break?**

Hilary: I pray that you comprehend the width, length, depth, and height of His love and the capacity of truth and strength that our good Father has to offer, especially in uncertain moments.

God knows what you need. If you place your trust in Him, His plan will become clear in His absolute perfect timing. There is a season of waiting, and there is a season of deliverance. Every single day we have to reset our priorities and trust that God will provide all that we need.

From Arrested to Resting in God's Promises

with Kachia Phillips

Kachia's story is beyond belief. Not only is she the survivor of human trafficking, but God's restoration and faithfulness is all over her story. She has a trust in Him that will inspire us all. Kachia is near and dear to me, and, after reading her story, she'll be near and dear to you too.

Hope: Tell us about when you started seeing God's fingerprints in your life.

Kachia: I was first trafficked as a teen. Then my sister married a man who ran an escort service. She asked me to move in with them and watch their kids at night. I also answered the phones for the escort service. When I saw all the material things they had, I wanted those nice things too. I ended up helping them open other escort services in the area and eventually opened up my own service.

Even through my mess, my faith never left me, even through all my trauma. After twenty-two years of living this way, I was exhausted. I'll never forget waking up one morning and feeling something shift within me. That happened to be the same day I was arrested.

I went into a store that morning with a friend. As soon as we walked out of the store, I was arrested. Crying, my friend asked me, "What do I need to do?"

I said, "Nothing. I'm tired." I had peace.

Hope: **It sounds like the Lord had been preparing your heart for this moment, giving you such peace.**

Kachia: Yeah, I was at peace at the time, even when I got in the back of the police car.

When I got to the jail, the chaplain gave me a Bible. I remember lying on the top bunk in my jail cell that night, raising my hands, and crying. I cried out to God and said, "Daddy, I need You to clean up my mess. I cannot do this anymore. I'm tired. If You are who You say You are, I'm going to lie right here until You come get me."

Hope: **That is so powerful. What do you think allowed you to be able to see God's fingerprints through your arrest and going to prison?**

Kachia: He knew I needed to see proof. He knew I was going to have to see something and it would have to be something big.

In those moments of doubt, even now, I'll ask Him, "I need You to show me that this is exactly what You want me to do. Give me some kind of sign."

When the chaplain gave me the Bible, a particular verse jumped out to me. It was John 8:32: "You will know the truth, and the truth will set you free." It was in that moment that I knew something big was getting ready to happen.

My friend Mary came to me in jail and said, "God sent me to come and get you." I gave her the phone number of a random bondsman I had never met. Twenty minutes later, the jailer came in and told me to gather my stuff.

Mary had called the bondsman, and he instructed the jail to let me out. The crazy part is Mary hadn't signed any paperwork or given the bondsman any money.

The jailer said, "He must really trust you because bondsmen never do this."

I said, "I don't even know this man."

At that point I was like, "Okay, God. I see You."

Hope: **What did the bondsman say? Why did he do this for you?**

Kachia: He was a fellow believer. He was a recovering alcoholic and had lost his wife. I know that the Lord picked him. I gave his number to my friend randomly, but God picked him.

Hope: **That is wild! What happened next?**

Kachia: Mary invited me to this women's retreat. The ladies at this event only spoke Spanish. Mary knew Spanish because she had been kidnapped and taken to Mexico for three years. She translated for me the entire weekend.

The pastor took us through a Bible study and had us write down the things that were strongholds in our lives. I started writing down things like low self-worth, prostitution, domestic abuse, and whatever else the Lord showed me at that time that I needed to be delivered from. Then, after I wrote mine down, the ladies surrounded me. They started praying for me and laying their hands on me ... all in Spanish.

Mary told me, "Call them out. Call them out."

I started calling each of the strongholds out in Jesus' name. Before I realized it, I was on the floor throwing up and coughing. It was like things were coming out of me, and they didn't want to come out. They didn't want to leave.

I lost my voice, and after I had called every single stronghold out in Jesus' name, I stood up and looked out the window and saw a bald eagle flying. I heard the Lord say, "It is finished."

I immediately thought again of John 8:32: "You will know the truth, and the truth will set you free."

When we left the retreat, I was sitting on the bus next to a little fifteen-year-old girl. She grabbed my head with her hand and put my head on her shoulder. It broke me. It was the most precious thing, and she said, "It's going to be okay."

That is exactly what I had always told everyone around me. Through all those years of trafficking, I had kept my faith for other people, but I had never had faith for myself. When I went home, I didn't desire anything from my past life anymore. All of those desires were gone, and they have been gone ever since.

When I reflect on this moment, I realize it was all about a complete surrender. I had to be so tired of everything—my husband, my friends, my family, all the people in my life who were toxic to me. I had to surrender every single bit of it to God.

I had to empty all the bad stuff out for Him to put the good stuff in. I like to call this the great exchange.

Hope: The great exchange? That is SO good. I'm excited for people to hear your story, a story that screams God's goodness and restoration. Share where you are today. What are some dreams on your heart?

Kachia: I'm a reentry program specialist for a nonprofit. I help men and women with justice barriers so they can find better jobs and be successful when they reenter society.

I love encouraging people, and part of that is telling my story to give people hope. I want everyone to know that they don't have to live under their strongholds anymore. I want them to know the verses in the Bible are true. Every word God says is true. Those who know God's truth will be set free!

I also help out in different recovery groups. I hear people say their name and then say their stronghold. For example, "My name is so and so, and I'm an alcoholic or drug addict." I want people to know that they aren't held back by that anymore. Through the blood of Jesus they can be set free, and they don't have to claim that ever again. That isn't their identity.

I promised God that if He rescued me, I would spend the rest of my life serving Him and helping others. I want to expose the truth. If we expose the truth and shed a light on the truth, more and more will be set free.

Hope: **What would your advice be to the person who is struggling to see God in their life?**

Kachia: Jesus loves you. He has a purpose and a plan for you. Life is about a daily surrender. We have to surrender our lives to Him over and over again.

Once I figured out that my life was not about me, something switched. Your life was never about you. It's all about God. Once you understand that, it all makes more sense and starts to click.

From OnlyFans to Following Jesus

with Rylin Utah

From the moment I met Rylin, I noticed how she listens intently and shares what the Lord has placed on her heart with compassion. God is doing something in her that cannot be stopped. As this book comes to an end, I believe Rylin's story will give you hope, faith, and trust in the Lord no matter what He is asking you to do.

I hope you'll read her story as an example of what it looks like to let go of the ways of the world and cling to the promises of God. As we see in Rylin's life, God will lead you to places you'd never imagine.

Hope: **Tell us how you let go of the way of the world and chose to cling to the promises of God instead.**

Rylin: When I was eighteen, my parents kicked me out of the house. I didn't graduate from high school. I didn't have a stable address, a car, or any source of income. I didn't even have my social security card or my birth certificate. I started working on OnlyFans, doing online sex work, because that was the only thing I could think of to start making money.

Other people saw that I'd started this, and I started getting so much hate and negativity. It made me feel so bad about myself because it felt like everyone was watching me fail. I was so ashamed about it, but I didn't want anyone to know I was struggling. So I acted like it was something I was excited about and wanted to do.

One day I went to church knowing that I didn't want to stay the same. I was looking for something that wasn't going to keep me in this miserable state I was in. I wanted to be freed from the lifestyle I had been living.

I didn't immediately quit OnlyFans when I started going to church. I had a hard time letting it go. Putting my faith in God wasn't easy.

I remember thinking, *I'm going to quit. God has got this.* Then I remember thinking, *I'm psycho … like, what am I doing? This is my only source of income. I can't walk away from this.*

With OnlyFans, I was earning really, really good money. That wasn't easy to give up, especially when my options were limited. I didn't want to lose the materialistic things I enjoyed.

When I met God, He changed my actions and taught me that He doesn't look at us as dirty. He doesn't see us as "bad." When we feel like this, that's the enemy trying to prevent us from finding God.

Getting out of my OnlyFans contract wasn't easy. My management told me I wasn't allowed to quit for three more months. I decided to stop sending them content. When I did this, my management team called and offered me a million-dollar deal. They wanted to give me a new account with a fake name, and they promised I would never have to show my face.

As tempting as that was, I declined the million-dollar deal and deleted my account. I had no backup plan. I lost my car, my house, and every other material thing I'd acquired. But it didn't matter. I knew that the plans God had for me were bigger.

I have so much contentment in my heart because God put value in my soul. He thinks that I'm worthy, and He wants to know me.

The more I get to know Him, the more I want to give up my life for Him. I no longer love the things this world has to offer. God fills me with love and joy and peace and patience and kindness and goodness and faithfulness and self-control. That's my testimony.

Hope: Wow! I have chills. You mentioned that you decided to go to church. Tell us a little more about what led you to go and what happened when you were there.

Rylin: I was in a hard season of my life. I had become so depressed, and I was having anxiety attacks. I decided to buy this crystal ring that was supposed to take away my anxiety. The second I put it on, I started having even worse panic attacks. I became consumed with fear, worried about what might happen if I lost the ring. I was having more anxiety with the ring than I'd had without it. Then, I started hearing voices and was being tormented all the time. I knew if I was hearing demonic voices, then there had to be a God.

I ended up texting one of my friends. We had been friends for a long time and found this mutual friendship in the fact that we were both depressed and wanted to die. We used to joke about killing ourselves, but one day we took it too far. We planned to jump off the Golden Gate Bridge. For some reason, I said, "Let's go to church first."

We went to a church in LA, and the pastor said, "I feel like some of you are thinking, *Oh, I just want to jump off the Golden Gate*

Bridge. News flash—this life isn't about you. Nothing about living here is about you. You're not supposed to be living for yourself."

This was our wake-up call, and we decided not to move forward with our plan. We were still depressed, and we were surrounded by a bunch of other twenty-year-olds who were drinking, doing drugs, and living for the world. I wasn't really in a place where I could grow my faith.

More time passed, and I found myself drunk in a club. I was very vocal about wanting to kill myself when a friend invited me to a Bible study. I left the club drunk and went to the study. This guy started telling his testimony there, and it sounded so similar to my testimony. We had grown up at the same time, moved to the same places, and had very parallel stories. So I sent him a direct message. I told the Lord, "If You're real, have him respond to my direct message." He never responded, so I went to another club after the Bible study and continued on with my life.

Another year went by, and I had only become more anxious and depressed. Nothing was helping me. I developed an eating disorder and was starving myself. I was scared all the time, and I really wanted to die. I don't know how to explain it other than I was horrified all the time to be alive. I had no peace.

So I texted my friend. I said, "Hey, can you pray for me?"

He said, "Why don't you come to a Bible study?"

I remember saying, "I don't want to do that."

He said, "Just come. Just come. Just come."

I went to this Bible study and was hanging out with everyone. I went through a lot of different forms of abuse growing up, so I was

very good at covering up and hiding what was really going on in my life.

It was almost the end of the Bible study, and one of the boys stood up. I'd never talked to him before. He'd never met me. He looked around and said, "Somebody here is being demonically tormented."

I was like, "I am!" I started sobbing. As I was crying, I said, "I'm so scared."

All of a sudden, everyone in the room was like, "You're not crazy. You're not crazy."

I had felt crazy for years.

These girls pulled me into a room, and they prayed with me. Without knowing my history, they started speaking things over me. They said that they saw me with a microphone. They saw me pulling girls out of sexual abuse and sexual assault. They asked me if there was anything hindering my relationship with God. I sat there and heard, "You're doing sex work."

I looked at the girls and I said, "I do sex work."

They had no idea. They were speechless. I think they looked at each other and said, "Oh."

They asked me if I wanted to be free, and I said yes. They encouraged me to build a relationship with the Lord and to let go of the things that were hindering my relationship with Him. They never told me to quit doing sex work. They were there for me. Loving me and accepting me exactly as I was.

I have never felt so seen and so understood in my life. For the first time, I felt like I wasn't a burden. I wasn't annoying. I wasn't crazy. And I wasn't alone.

My friends and I were still influencing, and we got invited to an influencer party. One of my friends asked me to go with her, and I was filled with anxiety. I was on the floor of a grocery store in LA having a panic attack when I decided to call one of the girls who had prayed over me the night before at the Bible study.

I didn't tell her why I needed her to pray for me. I simply asked that she pray, and she did. I got to the party, and they called out the person's name in line in front of me. Guess who it was. It was the girl who had prayed over me.

She told me that the Lord had told her she was supposed to go to this event. She thought it was to evangelize.

When I saw her, I felt protected for the first time in years. I heard the Lord tell me that I am with Him now and He is protecting me. It felt like someone was going to war for me and fighting for me. It didn't feel like I had to fight my own battles anymore.

Hope: That's so beautiful to me. The fact that she was in front of you is reminding me that He goes before us. Tell us what happened after this and where you are now.

Rylin: The church group loved me back into my original design. It was honestly the men in the group who really changed me. I was surrounded by a bunch of men who didn't want to sleep with me or follow my Instagram (where I was still posting very provocative photos). They actually started asking me why I was posting what I was posting.

My walk with the Lord has been a journey. The Lord became my teacher. As my love grew for Him, there were more and more things I was willing to lay at His feet.

I will share this next story so you can understand the transformation the Lord did in my life.

One day an old friend called me. This was a friend who'd gone to clubs and parties with me. We'd traveled together, and he had seen me at my worst. He asked how I was doing, and I told him how good I was doing and how I was going to church.

He laughed.

I asked, "Why are you laughing?"

He said, "If anyone would have asked me for the last two or three years who was the most depressed, suicidal, sad person I knew, I would have said you."

I sat there almost in delusion. I know how I felt was so real. I know I was hurting, and I know every single thing he said was true. Today, I can't even fathom the concept of feeling that way. It was like I didn't know that girl, the old me.

Right now, I'm on a tour traveling to ten states and twenty-two colleges to preach the gospel and evangelize. I am not even a glimpse of the person I was a year ago.

Hope: **Rylin, thank you for sharing your story with us! What encouragement do you have for the one who is waiting on the Lord to transform them and make them new?**

Rylin: Picture yourself staring at a pot of water waiting for it to boil. When you're staring at the pot of water, it seems like it's never boiling.

When you walk away from the stove, it starts boiling beyond belief. You ask yourself, "When did this happen?"

I want to relate this visualization back to sanctification. When we're staring at our problems and staring at the things we want to change, it doesn't feel like we're going anywhere. When we fix our eyes directly on Jesus, everything seems to just fall into place. Fix your eyes on Him!

One day you're going to look back and see how He transformed you. Take your eyes off the problems or the things you're waiting for and focus your eyes on Him.

From Adopted to God's Child
with Elia Glenn

The moment you meet Elia, you just know that something is different about her. She reflects Jesus in a way that is indescribable. She is wise beyond her years and loves God with her entire heart. It's impossible to be around her and not have a new perspective on life. She sees Him at work in the middle of all things, and I know her adoption story will make a lasting impact on you.

Hope: I'm so excited to hear your story. Tell us a little bit about you.

Elia: I'm a freshman at Geneva College, am the founder of the Delight Ministries chapter on the campus, and am from Pittsburgh, Pennsylvania. I was adopted by my mom, and as a single mom she raised me until I was nine. At that time, she remarried my dad, and I went from being the only child to having three brothers.

Hope: Did you always know you were adopted?

Elia: Yes, and my whole life I kind of had a vision of who my birth parents were. Even though I loved my adopted family, I always wondered in the back of my mind what my birth family members were like. For example, as a little girl, I obviously loved princesses, and I used to dream of being the long-lost daughter of a royal family.

Hope: Did you know anything about your birth parents growing up?

Elia: My mom told me the first name of my birth mother. She always prayed for her on Mother's Day and my birthday, so I always knew her first name. I never knew her last name though. My mom told me that she would tell me when I was eighteen.

My whole life I was counting down the days until my eighteenth birthday because I would finally be able to look up who my family was and know where I came from. When it was getting close to my eighteenth birthday, I had so much stuff going through my head. The week before, I said, "Hey, Mom, I'm so excited for my eighteenth birthday coming up. You're finally going to tell me the last name of my birth mother."

My mom said, "Elia, we need to talk." I didn't know what was going on. She told me that the reason why she'd never told me the last name and the reason why she still was not going to tell me on my eighteenth birthday was because she didn't want me seeing the mug shots of my birth mother.

She proceeded to share with me that my birth mother had been in prison multiple times for drugs and alcohol and that I was the product of a bar hookup. No one knows where my birth father lives since they just met at a bar. She then told me that she used to send my birth mom letters through the adoption agency and that my birth mom cut off all contact to her and didn't want to receive the letters with updates on me anymore.

Hope: I can't imagine how hard this was to hear. I'm so sorry, Elia.

Elia: It was really, really hard. In that moment, all the dreams and hopes I had about my birth mother since I was a little girl shattered. Instead, I heard she was a convict, and I was just a hookup at a bar. All of the anticipation that had been building up for me just fell down in that instant. I started thinking, *I'm a bastard. I'm unwanted. I'm a mistake.* I had all of these thoughts coming into my head, which were obviously a lie from Satan.

As I was having these thoughts, something that my youth group leader had said the week before in his lesson popped into my mind. He was talking about how our identity isn't defined by our past. He said that we, as children of God, are not defined by where we come from. I believe that God reminded me of his words to give me comfort in this moment.

This reminder allowed me to take hold of my thoughts and say, "No, this isn't true. This isn't my identity."

Hope: You are an inspiration, Elia. Your faith encourages me so much. What else did God teach you that you'd like to share with us?

Elia: God says that I'm beautiful. He says that I'm wanted and I'm loved. I really do feel like that's why God uses the word that we are *adopted* into His family because adoption is such a beautiful thing.

He chose us just like my mom chose me. I'm not my birth mother. I'm not. My identity has nothing to do with her and everything to do with how loved I am by God. That is what gave me so much peace and allowed me to be able to fight against all the lies that Satan wanted me to believe. I am the daughter of the King. I am the daughter of the Creator of the universe. The God who created the world around me is my Father. That is who I'm related to spiritually.

My adopted mom is such a strong woman. I can see everything that she's gone through to do for me. I really look up to her for that. I can't imagine what my life could have been if I was not adopted or if my birth mother had decided to keep me.

God is so good. I can see His hand all over my life when I start thinking about where I could have ended up. I might not have been a believer, which would have meant that I might not have been at Geneva to start a Delight chapter. When I reflect on how life could have been, I can see how God has proven to me that He sees me and that this is His plan for my life. The same is true for you, and I hope this helps you get through thoughts from the enemy making you question your identity and purpose. God doesn't make mistakes, and He sees every one of His children. I'm not a mistake, and nothing about your life is either. He knew what He had in store for me, and He knew what He had in store for you too.

From the American Dream to Living in Mozambique
with Brooklyn Howard

Crazy enough, Brooklyn and I grew up going to church together in a small town in Arkansas. She has always been full of joy, and I knew God had big plans for her. Brooklyn always envisioned doing mission work overseas but thought she would need more experience. God called her to do mission work in AFRICA right out of college and she shares wisdom that will set a fire in your heart. You'll be ready to close this book and run to what Jesus is calling you to NOW.

Hope: Brooklyn, I'm so excited to capture your story. Tell us about what God is teaching you through uprooting your life in America and moving to Africa.

Brooklyn: I never imagined in my wildest dreams that I'd be doing missions, especially in my twenties. I grew up in a small town in Arkansas and my family still lives there. From a very young age, I had a big interest in the medical field. I always considered going to med school.

As I got closer to college age, I learned more about physician assistants. I fell in love with that career and the idea of being a mid-level practitioner. I had several friends going to PA school, so I set myself on the track to go to PA school too. I took all the required chemistry and biology classes in college, and I studied hard. I

graduated with a degree in exercise science and a double minor in medical admissions and preprofessional health studies.

I set myself up to do health care and had this dream of one day, really far down the road, doing medical missions. I had gone on a few mission trips in high school and a longer-term mission trip in college, and I loved mission work.

The one thing stopping me was that I didn't feel equipped and felt I needed more training. I felt like I needed something more to offer than what I could bring to the table. I thought I'd go to this PA grad program, get more education, and then someday, God would use me overseas.

As I got closer to graduation, the rejection letters started coming in from PA schools, and the defeat crushed me. I felt like the Holy Spirit was telling me to take a year do some mission work. My immediate thought was, *Oh my gosh, that's just crazy. I'm from Arkansas. I just need to stay in Arkansas. I don't need to go anywhere else.*

I can't explain it, but I really felt this calling to do missions after I graduated college, even though it made no sense. So I finally gave into this big nudge, and I said, "Okay, I'll do it." Long story short, I got connected with a team here in Mozambique, and they needed someone to come teach their kids for a school year. Basically, I home-school their kids so they can continue their ministry. Let me remind you, I knew nothing about education and had no background. I thought I would do this for a year and then go to grad school.

Well, God just continued to shut doors for me to do anything in the medical field. I reapplied to so many schools and programs and

didn't get accepted to any of them. I also sought out opportunities here in Africa to practice medicine, and everyone turned me down.

I just remember being in a season of life when I was saying, "God, what do You want from me? I really want to serve You in the medical field, but You are just shutting all these doors." It was so discouraging.

One day, I got this call while I was here in Africa. They were like, "Hey, do you want to teach English?" And I'm like, "I mean … I speak English, but I don't know how to teach it." They said, "You can teach this English. You speak it." And I said, "Okay. Okay, Lord. If this is Your plan for me, then that's what I'll do."

I won't go into all the details, but the government messed up and gave me a five-year visa instead of a one-year visa. God put it on my heart to start an English program here. So here I am, three years into my five-year visa, and I've started an English program that is growing rapidly. I teach English through the Bible.

This is nowhere near where I thought I would be. If you had asked me five years ago where would I be in five years, I would have said, "I'm going to be a PA and practicing somewhere in Arkansas so that I'm close to my family and hopefully finding a husband." Here I am today, on the other side of the world, teaching English and doing something that I never ever dreamed I would do, but I'm absolutely loving it and having to trust God a lot to get through each day.

Hope: Brooklyn, this is crazy! How did you let go of how you thought life would look to step into God's will for your life?

Brooklyn: Jesus calls us to die to ourselves every day, and I feel like I am learning what that means by dying to the dreams I had and the things I wanted in life. I trust that God has something so much better for me. This is true for all His children. He has something so much better.

So what does that mean, to die to yourself? Our Western culture is so checkboxy and time oriented and self-oriented.

I mean, it's like, what can I do to make myself the best, to make myself better? What do I need to do?

What are the steps?

What are my next steps?

What are the next five years going to look like?

It's everywhere. It's in our conversations. People ask me when I'm going to get married and have a baby. I love these people, but these questions are frustrating. The mold that our society puts us in is that we have to do this and then this and then this. If you get out of that mold, it's terrifying, and people look at you like you're crazy. I mean, I've gotten some strange looks when I tell people, "Oh, well, I'm moving to Africa," or "I live in Africa."

That's just our culture. I think it's been good for me to step in a culture that's not time oriented and is very people oriented. When people ask me how long I'm going to be here, I respond and say, "Well, I'm going to be here till God calls me to do something else. It could be tomorrow. It could be when I'm in my sixties. I have no idea. I'm here now, and I just want to listen to what God has for me today."

I will say it hasn't been an easy battle. It's been an uphill battle. If you see my Instagram or read my newsletters, you may think, *Oh, wow, she's got this made. God opened these doors for her, and she moved to Africa, and now she lives this really cool life and speaks other languages and wears skirts all the time.* It's not like that. There are so many nights when I cry because I miss my best friends back home or because I am missing Christmas with my family. There are so many things I have missed out on because I chose to obey God's call and follow Him here, to Africa.

It hasn't been easy. So many hardships have come with living over here. There are physical hardships. Sometimes we don't have electricity or clean water. I'm surrounded by lots of diseases and poverty. On top of that, I'm missing my friends and my old lifestyle. I definitely went through several months when I just grieved the life I could have had, and I realized that I'm never getting my early twenties back. I think it's healthy to mourn those kinds of things, but at the same time, I can look at my life and I think, *Wow, I get to watch God working in people around me and in my own life. That is so much better than going to a concert with my friends or, you know, spending holidays with family. I would really love to do that, but watching God work in my life is worth it. It's worth everything I give up. It's worth dying to myself; it is worth myself. If I die tomorrow, this is what our lives are for.* To the woman who is contemplating if the call is worth the cost: it's worth it and God will provide.

God has given me such a beautiful community here with my mission team. I have such great support back home. I have this

awesome technology where I can FaceTime my friends, and I can stay in touch with them. God is right here. It's not like He calls you to this hard thing and then just leaves you high and dry. He's right there with you, and He gives you such beautiful blessings. If you open your eyes and let go of your plans, you'll see that God's plans are so much better than the things you've given up.

Acknowledgments

I've been waiting and waiting for the right time to sit down and thank those who have made this book possible, and I sit here once again struggling with the words. I remember sitting on a stationary bike every morning during my senior year of college writing down chapter ideas and dreaming of writing a book. My entire journey is one that points only to God.

First and foremost, God, I want to thank You. Thank You for filling me with Your Spirit and giving me the words and refining the message of fear on my heart to the fear of missing out. Thank You for giving us Jesus as our ladder into eternal life with You. Thank You for providing for me and my family and catching me every time I feel like I'm free-falling. Thank You for redefining my name and allowing me to find *new hope* in the promises You offer. My words will always fall short when it comes to thanking You. I hope and pray that this message brings You glory and honor. I know that any assignment You give me is more than I deserve, and it has been an absolute joy to get to write a book to help women see that there is no such thing as missing out when we are walking with You. My life is Yours, Lord. Do what only You can do through these pages. Thanks for letting me play a small role in this book.

Will—oh, honey—you are my rock! The last year of marriage has been one for the books. Our love has grown in ways I didn't know was possible. You've led our family to Jesus and loved me through some of our hardest days. You've kept me laughing and encouraged me to keep going on days when I wanted to give up. You're my safe place to land and the rock that keeps me steady as we navigate the good, the hard, and the in-between. Watching you be a dad to Remi has been everything I ever dreamed of and more. Thank you for the sacrifices you've made to make this ministry possible. The long hours you work and the things you do for our family don't go unnoticed. I can't believe God chose you to be my other half—my better half. I love you … beyond words.

Remi Claire Harris—you, my girl, bring so much joy to my life! I know you are just one right now, but this book wouldn't be possible without you. I always prayed that you would live up to your name and bring the remedy of God's light to the whole world. What God has taught me is that our mission often starts in our home first, and, baby girl, you have shown me God's bright light and healed me in more ways than you'll ever know. Getting to share stories about you from this season of life in these pages has been so sweet. You challenge me to wake up each and every day pumped to do life. You are strong, brave, and determined, and you light up an entire room. It doesn't matter who you see, you wave and smile. Your life has reminded me to see others how Jesus sees them. Thank you for bringing an indescribable joy to our family. Can't wait to watch you change the world!

Mom, getting to have conversation after conversation with you about this message has been so sweet. This book has brought our relationship to a new level. I'll never forget the conversations we've had. You challenge me to go deeper and give me the courage to put everything on my heart out there. I'll forever be grateful to you for helping me build a solid foundation for my faith. You lead by example—I'll never forget watching you on our back deck reading your Bible each and every morning before we went to school. Thank you for taking days off of work to watch Remi! I love you and can't wait for you to read these words.

Janis, your servant heart inspires me. You are steady, consistent, and always there. When you read these pages, I hope you know that all of these experiences have only been possible because of your support. You do whatever it takes to make sure our family has the support and love we need, no matter what the season is. This season just so happened to be a season where we needed lots of it. I aspire to show up like you. You're not afraid of leaning in, rolling up your sleeves, and making it happen. Thank you for all of the dinners you cooked so I could focus my time and energy on this message, and thank you for taking amazing care of our girly. I love you!

Dad, thanks for all of the "checking in on you guys" texts. You being there means more than the world. I wouldn't be where I am today without you! I'll never forget you telling me, "The answer is no until you ask"—you've always believed in me, which has often given me the faith that God can do what seems laughable and impossible. It is

so powerful to have an earthly father believe in you, and I can't thank
you enough for that gift. I love you!

Allen, thanks for keeping us laughing and working so hard to make it
all happen for the Harris crew. You're Will's go-to, which basically, in
a roundabout way, means you're my go-to. Thanks for always answer-
ing your phone on the first ring to get Will and us through whatever
life throws our way. You always stand ready to help us and jump
in—whether it be our garage door breaking or personal finance advice
or taking Remi Claire for a golf-cart ride to pet horses. We love you!

Ashtynne, Elia, Jackie, Kachia, Rylin, and Sarah, I sit here today
absolutely mind-blown by how God brought each of you into my life
THIS YEAR for such a time as this. I could go on and on about
every single one of you. The love each of you has for the Lord is truly
inspiring. Your stories elevate and celebrate God's goodness, faithfulness, and restoration. It is so sweet to do life with each of you. Forever
cheering you all on!

Brooklyn, it was an absolute joy getting to catch up and hear all that
God is doing in your life. It is so neat to have known each other our
entire lives and see all God has done. You inspire me to keep going
and remind me that no matter how you count the cost … the cost of
following Jesus is WORTH it. I love you!

Jaden, Hilary, and Trinity, the way the Lord orchestrated each of us
meeting is wild. The way you guys believe in the mission of Purpose

Doesn't Pause astounds me. Each of you brings something so different and unique to the table, and I still can't believe God brought me each of you. I'll never be able to thank you guys for bringing your God-given gifts and talents and time to this mission. You guys are the best teammates I could ever ask for. This is only the beginning! I can't wait to reflect back on this season and be able to say, "It was only God!" I'm expectant that He is at work right now and going to blow our minds. I love each of you SO much!

Susan and DCC team, thank you for believing that I had another message hidden in my heart that the world needed to hear. Thank you for letting me dream big dreams and locking arms with me to figure out a way to make it happen. You all are the dream team and I'm forever in your team's corner.

Julie, you get me. Thank you for helping me find the words and articulate this message on my heart for the world to read. Writing this book and knowing that you'd be holding hands with me on the next step kept me going. I'll never forget texting you that I was struggling and you encouraging me. You are humble, kind, and have a heart of gold. Thank you for using your God-given gifts to elevate the messages that God gave others for His glory. Your light shines bright.

I could write an entire book on all of the support, kindness, and encouragement from friends and family that have kept me going. The Lord has truly blessed me with people sprinkled all around

the world who believe in the assignment He has called me to. If you are reading this book, consider this a big ole hug—one of those hugs where it feels like you're reuniting with a long-lost friend after a few years. Thanks for being in my corner. I'm in yours! Much love.

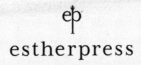

DAVID C COOK

JOIN US.
SPREAD THE GOSPEL.
CHANGE THE WORLD.

We believe in equipping the local church with Christ-centered resources that empower believers, even in the most challenging places on earth.

We are committed to spreading the gospel across villages, cities, and nations, trusting that the Word of God can transform lives and communities and bring light to the darkest corners.

David C Cook is a global ministry with a 150-year legacy, dedicated to this mission. When you purchase a book or donate, you're not just supporting a ministry—you're actively helping spread the gospel, discipling believers, and raising leaders in some of the world's most challenging regions.

We believe in the power of the church, in the power of Jesus, and that God is always at work, inviting people to join Him. Your support fuels our mission. Your partnership sends the gospel to places where it's most needed.

davidccook.org

estherpress

Books for Courageous Women

ESTHER PRESS VISION

Publishing diverse voices that encourage and equip women to walk courageously in the light of God's truth for such a time as this.

BIBLICAL STATEMENT OF PURPOSE

"For if you keep silent at this time, relief and deliverance will rise for the Jews from another place, but you and your father's house will perish. And who knows whether you have not come to the kingdom for such a time as this?"

Esther 4:14 (ESV)